MONGOLS, HUNS AND VIKINGS

MONGOLS, HUNS AND VIKINGS
NOMADS AT WAR

Hugh Kennedy

General Editor: John Keegan

CASSELL

For Alice, with love

Cassell & Co
Wellington House, 125 Strand
London WC2R 0BB

First published 2002

British Library Cataloguing-in-Publication Data
A catalogue record for this book is available from the
British Library.
ISBN 0-304-35292-6

Cartography: Arcadia Editions
Picture research: Elaine Willis
Design: Martin Hendry

Typeset in Monotype Sabon

Printed and bound in Italy by Printer Trento S.r.l.

Acknowledgements

I would like to thank Robert Bartlett for his help in putting me in touch with this project. I would also thank most warmly the Cassell team, Penny Gardiner, editor, James Ewing, editorial assistant, Elaine Willis, picture researcher, Malcolm Swanston, artist, and Martin Hendry, designer, for creating such an elegant volume.

HUGH KENNEDY
St Andrews

The classic nomad warrior, this Mongol horseman turns in the saddle to fire his bow to the rear – the 'Parthian shot'.

CONTENTS

KEY TO MAPS

Symbols on map

⚔ battle

🏰 castle or fortified town

Name style

SULTANATE OF DELHI Independent state

Thrace province

SARMATIANS major tribal group

Geographical symbols

🔶 urban area

——— road

——— river

- - - seasonal river

╌╌╌ canal

——— border

Military movements

➤ attack

⇢➤ retreat or conjectural movement

MAP LIST

CHRONOLOGY

The Huns

c. 370	Huns begin to move west from Central Asian steppes.
376	Goths defeat East Roman army at battle of Adrianople.
395	Death of Theodosius the Great and the division of the Roman Empire into East and West. Arcadius (395–402) is Eastern Emperor and Honorius (395–423) Western Emperor.
395–6	Winter: Danube freezes and Huns enter Balkans.
402	Theodosius II (402–50) becomes Eastern Roman Emperor.
c. 420	Huns attack Persia.
425	Valentinian III (425–55), Western Roman Emperor.
427–9	Aetius uses Huns to defeat Franks and Visigoths.
434	Attila becomes king of the Huns with his brother Bleda.
437	Treaty of Marga between Roman and Huns grants Huns massive tribute. Huns destroy the Burgundians at the instigation of Aetius.
441	Huns sack Naissus (Nis). Romans agree to Huns' demand that all land within five days' journey from the Danube should be left uncultivated.
445	Attila has Bleda murdered and becomes sole king of the Huns.
447	Huns invade Greece which is 'ground to dust'. Eastern Romans agree to pay Huns 2,100 pounds of gold per year.
448	Priscus' embassy to Attila.
450	Honoria asks Attila to save her from a loveless marriage. The warlike Marcian becomes Eastern Roman Emperor.
451	Attila decides to invade Western Roman Empire. 20 June: Huns defeated by Aetius and his allies at battle of Catalaunian Plains (Châlons-sur-Marne).
452	Huns invade Italy and sack Aquileia.
453	Death of Attila.
454	Valentinian III murders Aetius.
454–5	Battle of the Nedao results in break-up of Hunnic Empire.

The Arabs

c. 570	Birth of Muhammad.
622	Muhammad's *hijra* (migration) from Mecca to Medina.
624	First Muslim victory over Meccans at Badr.
626	Battle of the *Khandaq* between followers of Muhammad and the Meccans.
628	Byzantine Emperor Heraclius invades Persian Empire and sacks capital Ctesiphon (near Baghdad).
629	First Muslim raid on Jordan.
630	Muslims take Mecca.
632	Death of Muhammad. Accession of first caliph Abu Bakr (632–4).
633	Muslims complete subjugation of Arabian peninsula.
634	Accession of second caliph 'Umar (634–44). Khalid b. al-Walid marches from Iraq to Syria. Persians defeat Muslims at battle of the Bridge in Iraq.
636	Muslims defeat Persians at battle of Qadisiya. Muslims defeat Byzantines at battle of Yarmuk.
641	'Amr b. al-'As leads Muslim conquest of Egypt. Fall of Alexandria. Death of Emperor Heraclius.

Fall of Caesarea completes Muslim conquest of Syria and Palestine.

651 Death of last Sasanian shah Yazdgard III in north-east Iran.

661–750 Umayyad caliphs rule from Damascus.

670 Muslims begin conquest of Tunisia.

695 Muslims take Carthage and complete conquest of Tunisia.

708 Muslim armies reach Tangier and the Atlantic coast of Morocco.

711 Muslim armies invade Spain.

711–12 Muslim armies march through southern Afghanistan to invade Sind (Pakistan).

712 Muslims take Samarkand (Uzbekistan).

732 Muslim advance in France stopped by Charles Martel at battle of Poitiers.

The Turks

552 Turks replace Juan-Juan as rulers of Central Asian steppes.

568 Turkish mission to Constantinople to discuss silk trade.

583 Turkish Empire breaks up into eastern and western halves.

682–92 Khan Elterish reunites Turkish Empire in Central Asia.

745 Break-up of Turkish Empire in Central Asia.

833–42 Caliph al-Mu'tasim makes Turks the mainstay of the armies of the 'Abbasid caliphs.

869 Death of al-Jahiz, writer about the Turks.

1040 Battle of Dandanqan and entry of Ghuzz Turks into the Middle East.

1055 Ghuzz Turks take Baghdad. Seljuk Tughril Beg becomes sultan.

1063 Alp Arslan (1063–72) is sultan of Seljuk Turkish Empire.

1068 Romanus IV becomes Byzantine Emperor (1068–71).

1071 24 August: Turks defeat Byzantines at battle of Manzikert.

1072 Malik Shah (1072–92) is sultan of Turkish Seljuk Empire.

1157 Death of Sanjar, last of the great Seljuk sultans.

The Mongols

1170 Approximate date of birth of Genghis Khan.

1206 Great Kuriltay on the Onon river establishes Genghis Khan as ruler of all the Mongol peoples.

1209 Genghis Khan begins attack on Tangut Empire in western China.

1210 Genghis Khan forced to make peace with Tanguts.

1211 Kuriltay on Kerulen river decides on campaign against Chin rulers of northern China.

1214 Mongols take Chinese capital of Zhongdu (near Beijing).

1216 Genghis Khan destroys Merkit people who had rebelled against him in Mongolia.

1218 Muslim governor of Utrar (Kazakhstan) pillages caravan travelling under Genghis Khan's protection.

1219 Mongols begin conquest of north-east Iran.

1220 February: Utrar taken and sacked by the Mongols.
Death of Khwarazm Shah 'Ala al-Din.

1221 February: Mongols take and sack Merv.

1227 Death of Genghis Khan. Ogedei becomes Great Khan.

1231 Death of Jalal al-Din, son of the last Khwarazm Shah.

1236 Mongols attack Cuman nomads of southern Russia.

1237 Autumn: Mongols begin invasion of north-east Russia.
December: Mongols take Riazan.

1238 February: Mongols take Vladimir, capital of north-east Russia.

This painted stone (eighth/ninth century) from Ardre church on the Baltic island of Gotland gives a clear idea of how Viking ships were sailed and steered, which the archaeological evidence does not reveal. Note also the mounted warrior on the upper register, reminding us that most Viking battles were fought on land.

222222

	March: Novgorod saved from Mongols by spring thaw.
1239	Autumn: Mongols invade south-west Russia (modern Ukraine). December: Mongols take and sack Kiev.
1241	Spring: Mongol army returns to Volga steppes to await orders of the new Great Khan. 9 April: battle of Liegnitz. Mongols defeat Henry the Pious of Silesia. 11 April: battle of Mohi. Mongols defeat Hungarian army. December: Death of Great Khan Ogedei. 25 December: Mongols sack Gran (on the Danube, east of Vienna).
1251	Great Khan Mongke sends his brother Kubilai to attack China and Hülegü to attack Iran.
1256	Death of Prince Batu, invader of Europe and founder of the Khanate of the Golden Horde in the Volga steppes. Spring: Hülegü arrives in Iran. November: Hülegü takes Assassin strongholds of Maymun-Diz and Alamut.
1258	30 January: Mongols begin attack on Baghdad. 6 February: Mongols take Baghdad.
1260	Spring: Mongols take Aleppo. 3 September: Mongols defeated by Mamelukes at battle of 'Ayn Jalut.

The Vikings

789	First recorded Viking raid at Portland, Dorset.
793	Vikings raid abbey of Lindisfarne on the Northumberland coast.
795	First Viking raid on Ireland.
799	First Viking raid on western France.
814	Death of Charlemagne.
840 et seq	Division of the Carolingian Empire.
834, 837	Trading port of Dorestad on the lower Rhine sacked.
843	Vikings seize island of Noirmoutier near mouth of the Loire and make it their base.
844	First Viking raid on Spain reaches Seville.
859–61	Hastein and Bjorn lead raid through the Straits of Gibraltar to southern France and northern Italy.
865	Ivar and Halfdan lead Danish Great Army to attack East Anglia.
866	Vikings take York. Foundation of the Danelaw. Vikings leave the Seine after being paid massive tribute.
869	Vikings kill Edmund, last king of East Anglia.
873	Vikings take Repton, capital of Mercia.
885	Vikings besiege Paris.
889	Vikings driven from Seine valley by Odo, Count of Paris.
909–17	Edward the Elder of Wessex takes the Danelaw south of the Humber.
911	Charles the Simple makes a treaty with Rollo establishing duchy of Normandy.
c. 965	Harald Bluetooth and the Danes converted to Christianity.
991	Olaf Tryggvason of Norway defeats East Anglians at battle of Maldon.
995–1000	Olaf Tryggvason converts Norway to Christianity.
999–1000	Althing (Parliament) of Iceland establishes Christianity as the official religion.
1007	Svein Forkbeard of Norway begins to raid eastern England.
1013	Death of Svein Forkbeard and accession of Cnut.
1015	Brian Boru, king of Munster, defeats Vikings at Clontarf.
1018	'Great Army' dissolved.
1035	Death of Cnut.
1066	Last Scandinavian invasion of England under Harald Hardrada defeated at Stamford Bridge.

THE NOMAD PARADOX

A NINETEENTH-CENTURY ORIENTALIST PAINTER picks up the romantic view of the lone Arab guiding his caravan of camels through the desert. In reality Muhammad grew up in a world in which trading caravans were big business and commercial links meant that his message spread far beyond his homeland in Mecca and Medina.

THE NOMAD PARADOX

I<small>N THE HISTORY OF WARFARE</small> it has generally been the case that military superiority lies with the wealthiest states and those with the most developed administration. It is, after all, these states who can afford to train and pay the best soldiers and offer them the most advanced weapons and the most regular supplies. At least since the sixteenth century, finance and administrative efficiency have been key factors in military success.

The nomads who ravaged and sometimes dominated the lands of the Middle East, or, in the case of the Huns, central and eastern Europe, were an exception to this rule. Almost by definition, they did not have states and administrative apparatus, they were often dirt poor and entirely unversed in the arts of civilized

living. Yet their military prowess was undoubted and groups of nomads often put the armies of settled areas to ignominious flight. In this book I will try to offer some explanations for the 'nomad paradox'.

The mobility of the nomads was a major factor. Not only could they surprise an enemy by appearing when they were believed to be far away, or encircling them in battle so that their enemies suddenly realized that they were surrounded, but they could, if necessary, retreat with equal rapidity. All the groups described here had environments into which they could retire and into which their enemies could not follow: the Huns, Turks and Mongols had the great grasslands of eastern Europe and Asia, where lack of grain supplies and brutal weather put off all who were not accustomed to them; the Arabs had the deserts in which they alone could find their way and survive; while the Vikings had the sea, the element in which their superiority was unchallenged.

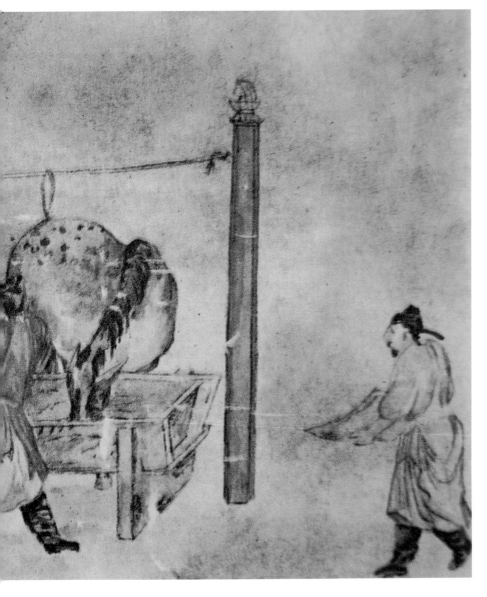

Mongols tending their horses. This fourteenth-century miniature by Jen Jen-fa, a Chinese official in the service of the Mongol khans, shows horses being fed and watered. In the early days of the Mongol conquests, the animals often had to fend for themselves, even digging through the snow with their hooves to find roots to eat.

With this command of the wilderness went the toughness and resistance to hardship which life in these areas brought. Both men and their horses could survive where the soldiers and animals of better endowed areas could not. This in turn made them highly mobile: not for them the lines of pack animals and creaking wagons which could slow the progress of an army down to a few miles a day. Nor did they have to worry about the loss of the supply train, since there was none.

All adult male nomads were warriors, or at least potential warriors. The insecurity of the wandering life and the lack of established authority meant that everyone had to be able to take up arms and defend themselves and their kin. There were no civilians in these societies. By contrast, the Roman Empire, the powers of the Islamic Middle East and, to a lesser extent, the Anglo-Saxon and Frankish kingdoms were all societies in which the military was a small specialized group in society: the vast majority of the population were civilians with neither

The Muslim army besieges the Byzantine city of Messina in Sicily which they captured in 842. This miniature, from an eleventh-century Greek manuscript, shows the Arab army wearing turbans and carrying spears and small round shields. There is no sign of any sophisticated siege engine.

arms nor the experience to use them. The overall numbers of nomads were usually much smaller than those of the settled peoples, but the percentage of those who were mobilized for military action was vastly greater.

Many nomads brought with them distinctive methods of fighting, above all mounted archery, the most effective fighting technique of the pre-gunpowder world. This was extremely difficult to counter using conventional military tactics. It was also very difficult to learn, since apparently only those born to the horse-based lifestyle could really master it. But there were other groups, the Arabs and Vikings for example, whose military skills and equipment were little different from those of their opponents and who relied on their mobility and hardiness to see them through.

In all nomad societies, leadership was based on skill and wisdom in warfare and hunting. Membership of a leading family or group might be an advantage, but even the highest-born incompetent would soon be found out. Such a meritocracy meant that nomad leaders were usually efficient and effective and enjoyed the respect of those they led. Men of obscure origins, like the Mongol Subedei, could rise to the highest positions. In contrast, settled and bureaucratic societies often entrusted military command to men who, although of high rank, lacked both experience and courage and were far from enjoying the confidence of their followers.

Camel train crossing the desert. The Arab nomad armies used camels for transport and as a source of milk and meat. Their ability to survive in waterless deserts gave Arab soldiers a mobility that their opponents could not match. In battle, however, the Arabs fought on foot or on horseback.

All these factors help to explain the military dominance of the nomads. Yet, with the exception of the Vikings, all the nomad explosions were the result of effective leadership. Most of these populations consumed their military energies by fighting with one another, which left them little or no energy with which to conquer lands other than their own.

This internecine strife only ended with the emergence of great leaders such as Attila or Genghis Khan, or when an ideology such as Islam bound the previously warring factions together. Only then were these formidable reserves of military energy unleashed on the outside world.

CHAPTER ONE

ATTILA AND THE HUNS

THERE ARE NO SURVIVING contemporary representations of Attila, which has allowed artists to let their imaginations run riot. In this illustration from a popular French history book of 1942, he is shown with a Mongol hat, lamellar armour, a strange pike-like weapon and a mangy and bedraggled mount.

ATTILA AND THE HUNS

O F ALL THE NOMAD PEOPLES discussed in this book, the Huns have probably left the most fearsome reputation. In a way they are synonymous with savagery and their vast hordes seem to overwhelm everything before them. To some extent this reputation is undeserved. The Huns appeared (and disappeared) in the course of less than a century and mass Hunnic invasions of the Balkans and western Europe lasted a much shorter time than that. However, these were dramatic and fairly well-documented years. The works of contemporary historians like Olympiadorus and Priscus survived, incorporated in later chronicles, so that subsequent generations could read in fascinated horror about these fierce people. In the English-speaking world, the theme was picked up again by Edward Gibbon; Attila and the Huns play a dramatic role in his *Decline and Fall of the Roman Empire*, a very widely read and admired work which shaped all the subsequent accounts of these turbulent years. But the notoriety of the Huns was established forever during the First World War when British propagandists, hoping to cash in on the ancient reputation of these people, began using the term 'Hun' to mean Germans. By this they hoped to evoke those ancient images of brutishness and barbarism to stir up hatred. In historical reality, of course, the epithet was entirely misplaced: the Huns were definitely not a Germanic people and if there is one consistent feature of Hunnic military activity it is their abiding hostility to the Germanic Ostrogoths, Visigoths and Burgundians.

The reputation of the Huns has not been improved by the fact that we have no Hunnic voices to speak to us. Whereas the Arabs have their poetry, the Vikings their sagas and the Mongols their *Secret History* to illustrate their society from the inside and according to its own set of values, there is no Hunnic literature. Indeed, apart from proper names, only one word of the Hunnic language seems to have survived. Instead we are dependent on the accounts of outsiders who regarded them with, at best, awestruck dread. Only the Priscus account of his mission to Attila's court, which itself only survives in fragments, is based on extensive first-hand observation. The Huns have had a bad press through the centuries but this may be in part because they have not been able to put their own point of view.

The origins of the Huns are shrouded in mystery, not just for us but also for contemporary observers, who frankly admitted that they had no idea where these people had appeared from. It was clear that they had come from the east and there was a persistent but improbable story recounted to explain how they were first encouraged to move west. According to this legend, the Huns and the Ostrogoths lived in

The English historian Edward Gibbon (1734–94) described the Hunnic empire in his famous Decline and Fall of the Roman Empire. *Based on classical sources, his account was the basis of the popular image of the wild and savage Huns which British propaganda tried to exploit during the First World War.*

neighbouring territory separated by the Strait of Kerch, which is the entrance to the Sea of Azov: the Ostrogoths in the Crimea on the western side and the Huns in the steppes to the east. However, neither group knew of the other's existence. One day a cow belonging to a Hun was stung by a gadfly and swam across the strait followed in hot pursuit by her master. He found himself in a rich and inviting land and when he returned to his own people he told them about it and they immediately moved to take it for themselves.

The historical reality seems to be that the Huns, a Turkic people from the Central Asian steppes, began to move west around the year 370 and attack the Ostrogothic kingdom in the area of the modern Ukraine. What caused this movement is unclear, but it may have been pressure from other tribes further east. The Ostrogoths were defeated again and again and forced to leave their homes and farms in panic. A vast number of them crossed the Danube into the Balkans, still ruled at this time by the Roman Empire. Here the fugitive Goths, in their desperation, inflicted a massive defeat on the Roman army at Adrianople

St Jerome, famous as an early Christian ascetic and translator of the Bible, is seen here in an imaginary portrait by the sixteenth-century Dutch artist, Rey Mersswaele. In his retreat in Bethlehem, Jerome heard and recorded first-hand accounts of the terrifying Hunnic raids on the eastern provinces of the empire.

in 376, when their cavalry ran down the last of the old Roman legions.

Now that their horizons were expanded there was no stopping the Huns. They raided the Balkans in the aftermath of the Roman defeat but also attacked the rich provinces of the east, coming through the Caucasus and Anatolia to pillage the rich lands of Syria. St Jerome, the translator of the Bible into Latin, was living as a hermit near Jerusalem at the time and he has left us one of the first contemporary accounts of their cruelty:

Suddenly messengers started arriving in haste and the whole east trembled for swarms of Huns had broken out from (behind the Caucasus). They filled the whole earth with slaughter and panic as they flitted here and there on their swift horses. The Roman army was away at the time and detained in Italy owing to civil wars ... they were at hand everywhere before they were expected: by their speed they outstripped rumour, and they took pity on neither religion nor rank nor age nor wailing childhood. Those who had just begun to live were compelled to die and, in ignorance of their plight, would smile amid the drawn swords of the enemy. There was a widespread report that they were heading for Jerusalem and that they were converging on that city because of their extreme greed for gold.

Jerome takes up a number of themes which were to echo through the centuries as people of the settled lands recounted with horror the arrival of nomad warriors: their speed and the fact that they caught unsuspecting people by surprise, their readiness to slaughter entire populations and their blatant and overwhelming greed for gold.

Another theme repeatedly taken up by observers of the Huns was their alleged ugliness. Ammianus Marcellinus, the late fourth-century military historian, who is one of our most important sources for the earliest stages of the Hunnic invasions, commented that they were 'so prodigiously ugly that they might be taken for two-legged animals or the figures crudely carved from stumps that one sees on the parapets of bridges', while Jordanes adds that they caused men to panic by 'their terrifying appearance, which inspired fear because of its swarthiness and they had, if I may say so, a sort of shapeless lump rather than a head'. These impressions probably reflect the eastern Asiatic features of the Mongols which made them clearly distinct from their Germanic rivals and neighbours (about whom the Roman sources do not make the same comments).

Their physical appearance was not made more attractive to the Romans by their clothes. These seem to

This skull of a Hunnic female has been deformed by binding. Like the binding of feet in China, this must have been thought to enhance female beauty. Roman sources, however, often comment on the ugliness of the Huns.

have been chiefly made of bits of fur and later of linen, presumably captured or traded because the Huns themselves certainly did not make their own textiles. Along with their ragged clothes and wearing their garments until they disintegrated was their habit of never washing. The effect of these on the fastidious Roman observers who encountered them may easily be envisaged. However critical, their enemies recognized their extreme hardiness for, as Ammianus Marcellinus observed, 'They learn from the cradle to the grave to endure hunger and thirst.' Not for them the heavy, slow-moving supply trains that delayed the movements of Roman armies for they carried all that they needed with them on their swift and sturdy ponies.

That the Huns were ferocious and very successful warriors is evident. It is less clear exactly why they were so. Our knowledge of both their tactics in battle and their equipment is very patchy. The main first-hand account, the work of Priscus, describes the Huns at leisure and pleasure but not at war, and the descriptions of battles from other sources are both later and too vague to be of much use. There is no known contemporary representation of a Hunnic warrior of the period. A few swords from the time, which may or may not be Hunnic, survive but there are no archaeological traces of the famous bows.

Ammianus Marcellinus, himself an experienced military officer, wrote of them in 392:

> When provoked they sometimes fight singly but they enter the battle in tactical formation, while the medley of their voices makes a savage noise. And as they are lightly equipped for swift motion, and unexpected in

Steppe ponies in the Central Asian grasslands. These tough and stocky animals gave the Huns and later nomads, like the Turks and Mongols, enormous mobility. They were used as riding beasts and sources of food, including the famous kumiz *or fermented mare's milk. In extreme circumstances, nomad warriors would bleed their animals and drink the blood.*

action, they purposely divide suddenly in scattered bands and attack, rushing around in disorder here and there, dealing terrific slaughter; and because of their extraordinary speed of movement, they cannot easily be seen when they break into a rampart or pillage an enemy's camp. And on this account, you would have no hesitation in calling them the most terrible of all warriors. At first they fight from a distance with arrows with sharp bone heads [instead of metal ones] joined to the shafts with wonderful skill. They then gallop over the intervening spaces and fight hand to hand with swords, regardless of their own lives. Then, while their opponents are guarding against wounds from sword thrusts, they throw strips of cloth plaited into nooses [i.e. lassos] over their opponents and so entangle them and pin their limbs so that they lose the ability to ride or walk.

Although Ammianus' account was derived second-hand from Goths who had fought against the Huns, the picture clearly shows them as nomad warriors in the military tradition which was to be followed by the Turks and Mongols. The emphasis on manoeuvrability, their role as mounted archers and use of lassos all form part of that tradition.

This mosaic from fifth-century Tunisia shows a nomad horseman, probably a Vandal, using a lasso to catch a deer. Like contemporary Hunnic warriors he has no stirrups, equipment which seems to have been unknown before the end of the seventh century.

As with all steppe nomads, observers were struck by their attachment to their horses. Jerome says that they ate and slept on their horses and were hardly able to walk on the ground. Ammianus Marcellinus noted that they were 'almost glued to their horses which are hardy, it is true, but ugly, and sometimes they sit of the woman-fashion (presumably side-saddle) and so perform their ordinary tasks. When deliberations are called for about weighty matters, they all meet together on horseback'. The Gaulish aristocrat Sidonius Apollinaris (d. 479), who must have seen Hunnic mercenaries on many occasions, notes that their training began

very young. 'Scarcely has the infant learned to stand, without its mother's help, when a horse takes him on his back. You would think that the limbs of the man and horse were born together, so firmly does the rider always stick to the horse. Other people are carried on horseback; these people live there.' Being well versed in classical mythology, he goes on to compare them with the mythical centaurs, half man and half horse. Commentators on nomad warriors are almost always impressed by this connection with their horses. No matter how early sedentary people learned to ride, or how well trained they were, they never seem to have acquired the mastery of horses that the nomad peoples had. This mastery always gave them the advantage in endurance and in the art of mounted archery which others could never attain.

The late Roman military tactician Vegetius whose book *Epitoma rei militaris* (Handbook of Military Science) is one of our main sources on the late Roman army, discusses the horses of the Huns and how they differed from the Roman ones. He describes them as having great hooked heads, protruding eyes, narrow nostrils, broad jaws, strong and stiff necks, manes hanging below the knees, overlarge ribs, curved backs, bushy tails, strong cannon bones, small rumps and wide-spreading hooves. They have no fat on them and are long rather than high. He adds that the very thinness of these horses is pleasing and there is beauty even in their ugliness.

This votive plaque from Khotan, an oasis kingdom on the Silk Road between China and Iran, shows mounted horsemen who may well represent early Turkish warriors bringing tribute to the Khotanese.

Apart from their physical appearance, like little ponies compared with the larger and more elegant Roman horses, what impresses Vegetius most is their toughness. He notes their patience and perseverance and their ability to tolerate extremes of cold and hunger. Vegetius was concerned at the decline of veterinary skills among the Romans of his day and complains that people were neglecting their horses and treating them as the Huns treated theirs, leaving them out on pasture all year to fend for themselves. This, he says, is not at all good for the larger and more softly bred Roman horses. There is an important point here: Roman horses needed to be fed and so the army had to carry fodder with it; Hunnic horses, by contrast, lived off the land and were used to surviving on what they could find. This gave them an enormous advantage in mobility and the capacity to travel long distances without resting. It was one of the secrets of their military success.

The question of whether the Huns used stirrups remains doubtful. We can be certain that stirrups were unknown in classical antiquity. We can also be certain that they were widely known in east and west from the eighth century onwards.

Although dating from around 500 BC, almost a thousand years before the height of Hunnic power, this bronze of a Scythian warrior shows that the tradition of mounted fighters was already well established in the Central Asian steppes.

The evidence for the intervening period is very problematic. There are no representations of horsemen using stirrups from the Hunnic period, nor have any metal stirrups been found in graves. If they had used a new and unfamiliar device like this, it seems most unlikely that Priscus and other classical commentators would have neglected to mention (and copy) this. It is therefore extremely unlikely that they had metal stirrups. It is possible that they may have had fabric or wooden stirrups, both of which are attested for in later periods, but again, the fact that these are not mentioned in sources makes it improbable. Mounted archers such as Scythians and Sarmatians, who preceded the Huns, were able to shoot from the saddle without the stabilizing effect of stirrups, and there is no reason why the Huns should not have done likewise. Indeed, the absence of stirrups for both sides would simply have emphasized the superiority of Hunnic horsemanship.

The Huns did not use spurs either but urged their horses on with whips; whip handles have been found in tombs. Gold and silver saddle ornaments discovered in tombs make it certain that some wealthy men rode on wooden saddles with wooden bows at front and rear to support the rider. Common sense suggests, however, that many poorer Huns must have made do with padded cloth or skin saddles or even have ridden bareback. Their most characteristic weapon was the bow. This was the short, but very powerful composite bow, perhaps 5 feet or more in length, made from wood, bone and sinews. The range would have been 200 to 300 yards, the maximum effective range of any medieval bow. In the early days at least, the arrowheads were made of bone, not iron. All the materials could be found on the steppes and the bow was the Hunnic instrument par excellence. Like the Turks and Mongols of later centuries, whom they so much resemble, it was their abilities as mounted archers that made them so formidable in battle. Better equipped Hunnic warriors would also have had swords and it is clear that Attila wore his sword even in the comparative safety of his own compound. Swords and their scabbards, like saddles, could be expensively decorated. Unlike the bows, which were peculiar to the Huns, the swords seem to have followed the standard Roman and Gothic forms, with short hilts and long, straight blades.

Confused by their speed, and perhaps hoping to account for their military success, contemporaries often gave very large numbers for armies of Huns: Priscus is said to have claimed that Attila's army in 451 had 500,000 men. If this were true, it would certainly explain their successes in battle but, in reality, these numbers must be a vast exaggeration. As we shall see when considering the Mongols, limitations on grazing for the animals must have placed severe restrictions on the numbers of Huns who could work together as a unit. Even in the vast grasslands of Mongolia, it is unlikely that Mongol gatherings ever numbered much more than 100,000: in the more restricted areas of the Balkans and western Europe numbers must have been much smaller. Before they invaded the Empire, the Huns, like other nomads, probably lived in fairly small tenting groups, perhaps 500–1,000 people, who kept their distance from their fellows so as to exploit the grassland more effectively. Only on special occasions or to plan a major expedition would larger numbers come together and even then they could only remain together if they had outside resources. The image of a vast, innumerable swarm of Huns covering the landscape like locusts has to be treated with some scepticism.

The late Roman Empire was a society based on walled towns and the Huns soon developed an impressive capability in siege warfare. This was surely not something they brought with them from the steppes. They almost certainly employed engineers who had learned their trade in the Roman armies but now found themselves unemployed and looking for jobs. The Huns were much more successful than previous barbarian invaders had been at reducing cities. This was especially important in the Middle Danube area around modern Serbia, where cities which had successfully held out for many years were reduced to uninhabited ruins. Sometimes, as at Margus, betrayed by its bishop, this was the result of treachery, but on other occasions the Huns were able to mount a successful assault. Priscus gives a full account of the siege of the city of Naissus (modern Nis in Serbia) in 441. While the narrative certainly has echoes of classical historians, especially Thucydides (for Priscus was an educated man and keen to show it), the description probably reflects the realities of siege warfare at the time:

Since the citizens did not dare to come out to battles, the [Huns], to make the crossing easy for their forces bridged the river from the southern side at a point where it flowed past the city and brought their machines up to the circuit wall. First they brought up wooden platforms mounted on

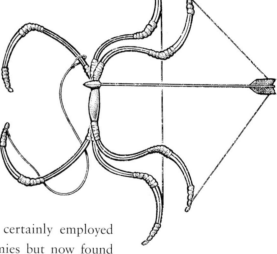

SHORT COMPOSITE BOW

This illustration shows the short composite bow of wood, horn and sinew, held together by animal glue. All the materials were obtainable in the steppe lands of Inner Asia. Curved bows like this were immensely powerful and short enough to be fired from horseback.

wheels upon which stood men who shot across at the defenders on the ramparts. At the back of the platform stood men who pushed the wheels with their feet and moved the machines where they were needed, so that [the archers] could shoot successfully through the screens. In order that the men on the platform could fight in safety, they were sheltered by screens woven from willow covered with rawhide and leather to protect them against missiles and flaming darts which might be shot at them. When a large number of machines had been brought up to the wall, the defenders on the battlements gave in because of the crowds of missiles and evacuated their positions. Then the so-called 'rams' were brought up. A ram is a very large machine: a beam is suspended by slack chains from timbers which incline together and it is provided with a sharp metal point. For the safety of those working them, there were screens like those already described. Using short ropes attached to the rear, men swing the beam back from the target of the blow and then release it, so that by its force, part of the wall facing it is smashed away. From the wall the defenders threw down wagon-sized boulders which they had got ready when the machines were first brought up to the circuit. Some of the machines were crushed with the men working them but the defenders could not hold out against the large number of them. Then the attackers brought up scaling ladders so that in some places the walls were breached by the rams and in other places those on the battlements were overcome by the numbers of the machines. The barbarians entered through the part of the circuit wall broken by the blows of the rams and also by the scaling ladders set up against the parts which were not crumbling and the city was taken.

WHEELED SIEGE TOWER

The Huns seem to have mastered Roman siege technologies rapidly, probably from deserters from the Roman armies. Priscus' account of the siege of Naissus describes them using wheeled siege towers and battering rams suspended from chains.

The attackers were using siege towers and battering rams but they do not seem to have had any artillery to fire stones at the walls or into the city. Later conquerors, notably the Mongols, were to use such catapults to great effect. In contrast, the Mongols do not seem to have used wheeled siege towers, at least in their Asian campaigns.

In addition to the machines, Attila was evidently prepared to sacrifice large numbers of men, probably prisoners or subject peoples, in frontal assault. The results were very impressive and most of the major cities of the Balkans, including Viminacium, Philippopolis, Arcadiopolis and Constantia on the Black Sea coast fell. Attila's campaigns mark the effective end of Roman urban life in much of the area.

One feature which marked out the Huns and other nomad warriors from the settled people was the high degree of mobilization among the tribesmen. When Priscus, a civil servant who accompanied the East Roman ambassador to Attila's court, was waiting for an audience with the great man, he was talking to a Greek-speaking Hun who gave him a lecture on the virtues of the Huns and Hunnic life as opposed to the corrupt and decadent ways of the Romans. He explained:

> After a war the Scythians [i.e. the Huns: Priscus uses the ancient Greek term for steppe nomads] live at ease, each enjoying his own possessions and troubling others or being troubled not at all or very little. But among the Romans, since on account of their tyrants [i.e. the emperors] not all men carry weapons, they place responsibility for their safety in others and they are thus easily destroyed in war. Moreover, those who do use arms are endangered still more by the cowardice of their generals, who are unable to sustain a war.

DEFENSIVE SHIELDS

Priscus describes how Hunnic archers were protected by screens covered with hides as they launched their arrows against the city walls.

BATTERING RAM

This is a simpler sort of battering ram where the assailants are protected by a mobile shelter covered with hides.

This passage forms part of a speech which is really a sermon on the virtues of the 'noble savage' lifestyle and Priscus attempted, rather lamely, to counter his views. But the Hun was making an important point about the enduring difference between the nomad society in which all adult males bore arms and a settled population who relied on a professional army. In absolute terms, the Huns may never have been very numerous but because of the high degree of participation in military activity, they could field a large army. They were, in fact, a nation in arms.

The story of the Huns may be divided into two distinct phases, the period before Attila and Attila's reign with a brief coda after his death.

After their first spectacular raids, men in the Roman world soon began to see the Huns as possible allies or mercenaries. In the fifth century, the Roman Empire in the east, with its capital at Constantinople and what was left of the Roman state in the west (ruled from Ravenna in north-east Italy) were constantly looking for new sources of soldiers. The feeble Western Emperor Honorius (395–423) once gathered a force of 10,000 Huns but had great difficulty in feeding them even for a single

A gold coin of the Western Roman Emperor Honorius (395–423). His long reign saw the increasing feebleness of the empire in the face of barbarian invasions. The failure of the emperor to lead armies in person allowed military commanders like Aetius to assume enormous power.

This sixth-century mosaic from Sant' Apollinare in Classe shows the fortified port of Ravenna in late antiquity. It was from here, rather than from Rome itself, that the feeble and corrupt emperors Honorius and Valentinian III (425–55) attempted to rule the Western Empire.

campaign and they soon dispersed. They could not simply be incorporated into the Roman armies as other barbarian *foederati* had been before them: the nomad lifestyle meant that it was like trying to herd cats. They would only follow leaders they respected, rather than obey orders without question.

Their role as soldiers in Roman Gaul was connected with the enigmatic personality of Aetius. Aetius has some claims to be considered as the last great Roman general in the West and as a heroic figure, striving against the odds, to preserve something of past glories in a very violent and confusing environment. At the same time he played complex political games to ensure his survival, not just against barbarian invaders but against the imperial court in Ravenna, where hostile politicians often sought to undermine him. From the 430s Aetius saw the Huns as useful potential allies. He had, we are told, been a hostage among the Huns when he was a child and so had the advantage of speaking their language and gaining an intimate knowledge of their ways.

Aetius recruited Huns to secure his own position in Gaul. Essentially, he and his lieutenant, the *dux* Litorius, employed Hun soldiers to defend the Romanized landowners of Gaul against their enemies, the Visigoths of Toulouse and the discontented peasants, known as the Bagaudae, who led guerrilla resistance to the increasing demands of landlords and states. In 437 Aetius famously persuaded the Huns to annihilate the Burgundians, a Germanic people who had a kingdom of sorts in the middle Rhine area. This massacre was remembered in history and myth and seems to have been the historical origin of the legend of the massacre of the Niebelungs which Wagner was later to make famous in opera. The Huns were far from invincible, however, and in 439 the Visigoths of Toulouse showed their power by defeating Litorius' attempt to take the city and killing the *dux* himself. Throughout this time, the Huns in Gaul acted as mercenary soldiers and, as far as we can tell, they had no territorial or political ambitions in the region.

All this changed with Attila's rise to power. It was Attila who gave the Huns a clear identity and made them, briefly, into a major political power. After his

A Visigoth foot soldier from an eleventh-century Spanish manuscript. In Gaul, Attila and his Huns were opposed by the Visigoths, a Germanic tribe that had already established a kingdom based on Toulouse.

death, they disintegrated with remarkable speed. The Huns had had kings before Attila. Around 420 we hear of one Rua and his brother Octar. However, as with many other nomad groups, the power of the king seems to have been very limited and real authority lay with chiefs of much smaller groups who were largely autonomous and did very much what they liked. Perhaps it was only when dealing with outside powers, notably the Eastern and Western Roman Empire, that the kings had a leadership role. In 434 Attila became king, ruling initially with his brother Bleda.

His predecessor Rua, seems to have been planning a major attack on the Eastern Empire but this was aborted because of his death. The Eastern Romans, preoccupied with wars against the Vandals (a Germanic tribe) in North Africa and the Persian Empire in the east, were anxious to secure their northern border. In 435 a Roman embassy, led by a Gothic soldier and a Roman diplomat – a typical division of labour at that time – met Attila at Margus (on the Danube just east of modern Belgrade). The negotiations took place on horseback outside the city walls. For the Huns, it was natural to do business without dismounting; the Romans, however, would have much preferred to have got off their horses and relaxed their aching limbs, but to save face they too remained on horseback. Attila's demands were not for territory but for money payments. Eventually it was agreed that the Romans would pay him the vast sum of 700 pounds of gold per year. It was also stipulated that the Romans would not receive or protect anyone fleeing from Attila's anger and that the Huns should have open access to markets.

This treaty established the Hunnic monarchy on a new basis. We can have no doubt that these large sums of gold were to be paid to Attila. This completely changed his relationship with the lesser tribal chiefs for he was now the source of patronage and all good things. If they wanted to be rewarded, the chiefs would have to obey Attila's orders. Now, probably for the first time, the Huns had a king with real authority. The provision about not sheltering fugitives from Attila's rule

A sixth-century mosaic from Carthage shows a Vandal nobleman going hunting. Hunting always played a major role in the lives of nomad warriors, serving as both a source of food and an excellent military training.

was also important because it meant that his enemies among the Huns – and there must have been some – had no safe hiding place, even if they fled to the enemy. The returned fugitives were usually executed immediately, often by impaling. The clause about markets was also important: if the Huns had all this money, they needed to have somewhere to spend it. It is usually assumed that all the Roman material goods and luxuries which Priscus saw when he visited Attila's camp were the results of raiding and pillaging. In fact, they may have been purchased quite openly – the product of extortion rather than looting.

Fortified by this regular income, Attila established himself as sole ruler of the Huns. As long as the East Romans kept paying, he was content to be a comparatively peaceful neighbour. However, there were times when the tribute was not delivered, either because the imperial government did not have the money, or because it believed that it was strong enough to defy him. When this happened, Attila's wrath was vented on the unhappy cities of the Balkans. In 440 Viminacium was sacked and depopulated to the extent that it was still a ruin a hundred years later. In 443 negotiations broke down again and Naissus was taken. This was a bitter blow for the prestige of the Roman Empire for Naissus had been the birthplace of the great emperor Constantine and he had endowed the city with many beautiful buildings. When Priscus and his companions passed that way five years later, they found the city depopulated, the great buildings in ruins and the country outside the walls still littered with the bones of the unfortunate inhabitants. Clearly Attila used terror and massacre with the same ruthlessness that Genghis Khan was to display some eight hundred years later. Nor did he stop there: he led his armies along the main road to Philippopolis (Plovdiv) where, in a classic nomad manoeuvre, he surrounded and largely destroyed the Roman army. Like many conquerors after him, however, he knew he did not have the skills or resources to attack the great walls of Constantinople. When peace was eventually renegotiated, the price, already high, had gone up threefold: the Romans were now required to pay a huge 2,100 pounds of gold per year. When this was not paid in 447, Greece was invaded and 'ground to dust'.

It was in response to this that Priscus' mission set out to treat with Attila. This embassy is of great importance because Priscus, who was essentially a civil servant sent along to assist Maximinus, leader of the delegation, left a first-hand account of the trip. In fact the mission was dogged by duplicity from the start. Maximinus and Priscus went in good faith to negotiate peace with Attila. They were accompanied, however, by an important Hun called Edeco who had come to Constantinople to open discussions. The eunuch Chrysaphius believed that he had persuaded Edeco, while in the capital, to murder his master in exchange for the promise of a luxurious life in Constantinople. In fact, Chrysaphius was too clever by half. On his return Edeco had privately decided to reveal all to Attila.

Priscus and Maximinus continued on their journey, unaware that their mission had already been sabotaged in this way. And it is as well for us that they

*The massive land walls of
Constantinople, built by the
emperor Theodosius II
(402–50) and strengthened
by subsequent rulers,
protected the city against
nomad invasions even when
all the surrounding
countryside was lost. Attila
himself never dared to
challenge them. Not until
the Fourth Crusade in 1204
were the walls finally
breached.*

did, for Priscus' account is the only detailed first-hand description we have of the Hunnic court. After passing through the ruin of Naissus, they reached the border on the Danube. Here they had a first glimpse of the new environment they were entering. They were ferried across the great river in dugout canoes made of a single tree trunk: it was already a different world from the Mediterranean where great merchant ships carried tons of grain from Egypt to Constantinople and cargoes of silk from Syria to the south of France.

They were now in the vicinity of Attila's camp but he – not surprisingly given the intrigue he knew was afoot – did not welcome them at all warmly. Priscus and Maximinus, unaware of the plot, were very disconcerted by this. When they were eventually allowed to greet the great man, he was furious with them. The ostensible cause of his rage was the fact that the Romans had not handed over some Hunnic fugitives. Attila was convinced that some of his own people were among the Romans and perhaps plotting his downfall very seriously: he would not, he said, 'allow his own servants to go to war against himself, even though they were unable to help those who had entrusted to them the guarding of their own land. For what city or fortress', he went on, 'had ever been saved by them

EMPIRE OF THE HUNS *c.* 451

This map shows the approximate area of Hunnic dominance at the time of Attila's death in 451, with the western and southern frontiers along the Rhine and Danube. In reality, the Empire lacked firm borders. The Huns made frequent incursions to the west and south and the borders to the north and east are largely conjectural.

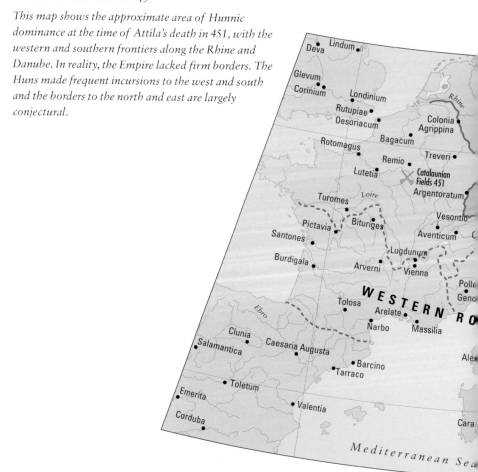

after he had set out to capture it?' It was, in fact, an insult to his dignity, rather than a military threat, that any Huns should serve the Romans and mercenaries against him.

After this unsatisfactory meeting, the Romans trailed after Attila as he moved north. The Huns were travelling with many of their possessions in wagons and rafts, as well as the dugout canoes which had to be assembled at the river crossings. The going was tough and one night the envoys lost much of their baggage in a terrible storm. They were saved by the kindness of the local people and observed the first signs of the surprisingly important role that women played in Hunnic society. Among the horse-nomads of the steppes, be they Huns, Turks or Mongols, women enjoyed much more freedom than they did among the settled peoples of the Roman world, let alone the world of Islam. After the storm they came to a village which was ruled by a woman who helped them retrieve their baggage and dry out. They were also offered beautiful young women with whom to enjoy themselves. The pious Priscus says that they entertained the ladies but did not take advantage of their favours. Sexual hospitality is a tradition not infrequently encountered in travellers' tales from the steppe regions. It may well

Empire of the Huns *c.* 451

——— border between Western and Eastern Roman Empires 395

- - - provincial border

have become an exaggerated myth and, of course, the writers always claim to have made their excuses. When the Romans left the village, they presented gifts that were available in the Mediterranean region but which were unobtainable in this part of the world, including dates and pepper from India.

As they continued north into the wilds, they met some ambassadors from the Western Roman Empire, who were also attempting to secure a firm and lasting peace from the great man. No doubt they found they had a lot in common, and much to talk about, but at the same time, there must have been some uneasy rivalry: if Attila made peace with the Eastern Romans, then the West would suffer next, and vice versa.

Finally they reached Attila's base, which Priscus describes as a 'very large village'. The Huns must originally have lived in tents, probably round felt ones similar to the yurts and gers of modern Central Asia; but for his permanent base, Attila had abandoned these and both his own palace and those of his leading nobles were constructed in wood. Nor were they simple log cabins, for the wood was planed smooth, and the wooden wall which surrounded them was built with an eye 'not to security but to elegance', though it was also embellished with towers. The only stone building was a bath-house, constructed on the orders of one of Attila's leading supporters, Onegesius. He had had the stone imported from the Roman province of Pannonia across the Danube. It was built by a Roman prisoner of war who had hoped to secure his release after the job was done. Unhappily for him, he had made himself indispensable and was kept on to manage the bath-house. The exact location of Attila's village unfortunately remains a mystery and no traces of it have been found; but it probably lay a short distance east of the Danube, in northern Serbia or southern Hungary.

The envoys were entertained in a series of dinner parties. The first of these was with Attila's senior wife, Hereka. Her house was of finely carved wood set on stone bases (to keep them from rotting). There were felt and woollen carpets on the floor and Priscus found his hostess reclining on a couch while her handmaids worked at embroidery and other domestic tasks. It is interesting to note that the 'queen' has her separate household and entertains foreign ambassadors without her husband or, as far as we know, any other men being present. When the Spanish ambassador, Clavijo, reached the court of Tamerlane at Samarkand, a thousand years later in 1405, he too was entertained by Tamerlane's wife and other women in the same way.

Priscus saw the great man around the compound and noted the awe in which he was held, but the setting was very informal, Attila moving freely among the people and listening to petitions. When Priscus arrived in the village, the young women came out to greet him and processed in front of him. His first meal was taken on horseback. It was all very different from the seclusion and hierarchy of the court back home in Constantinople.

The climax of the visit was a dinner party with Attila himself. The feast was stage-managed to accentuate the king's power but also his simplicity. Chairs were

THE ROUND YURT OR GER

This remains the typical tent of Central Asian nomads to the present day. It is likely that the Huns used very similar structures. Mounted on a wooden frame and covered with thick felt to keep out the bitter winter winds, they can be carried on animals or carts.

arranged in lines around the edge of the room with little tables in front of them, the guests seated according to their ranks. Attila sat on a couch with Onegesius on one side and two of his own sons, silent and respectful on the other (this seems to have been an all-male occasion). Behind his couch, concealed by rich linen curtains was the bed on which he slept. Priscus did not find the king physically impressive; but although short and squat with a large head and widely spaced eyes (unlike the nineteenth-century images of the mighty warrior), he had an undeniable air of authority. Toasts were drunk, each of the guests having their cups refilled by their own waiters. The platters of food were brought round and placed on the small tables.

Attila distinguished himself from the rest of the company by his simplicity of dress and manner. 'Neither the sword which hung by his side, nor the fastenings

This modern Kazakh yurt shows how snug and domestic the interior of one of these tents can be. Attila himself must have lived in much grander accommodation and Priscus' account describes him in a wooden palace, but many of his followers must have lived in structures like this.

The portrait of the empress Theodora (500–548) and her ladies from Ravenna shows the glittering splendour of the late imperial royal household. Honoria, the frustrated sister of the emperor Valentinian III, who appealed to Attila to rescue her, would have lived in such a gilded cage.

The image of Attila was used extensively by later artists. In this late nineteenth-century advertisement for meat extract (below) he is a symbol of virility and hardiness. In Benedetto Bofigli's fifteenth-century Italian image (opposite), he looks very much the Latin king. In fact, descriptions suggest that Attila was short and squat with a large head and strongly Asiatic features.

of his barbarian boots nor his horse's bridle was decorated, unlike those of the other Huns, with gold or precious stones or anything of value.' He ate off a wooden platter and drank from a wooden cup while the guests used gold and silver; they ate bread and other prepared dishes, he contented himself with plain meat. His clothing was plain and just like that of everyone else except, as Priscus sniffily observes, 'his was clean'. His behaviour was as dignified as his appearance: while his court laughed uproariously at the antics of a buffoon, he maintained an aloof silence. The banquet continued late into the night, with much drinking and singing of old battle songs, though the envoys took their leave long before it was over. The images are very striking. The barbarian chief impresses not by any nouveau-riche display of wealth but by his simplicity. Nor does he attempt to overawe the envoys with a display of military strength or by parading his army. At the same time, no one was left in any doubt where power lay or of the riches at Attila's disposal.

More days of dinner parties followed before the envoys were allowed to leave. Attila seems to have accepted that Maximinus and Priscus were innocent of the conspiracy against him which had cast a shadow over the arrival of the embassy. Priscus' mission paved the way for another, led by Anatolius in 450 when peace was finally secured and the Eastern Empire saved for ever, as it turned out, from Attila's wrath.

In 451 Attila decided on a complete change of direction. For reasons that we

ATTILA FLAGEL:DEI

do not completely understand, he chose to leave the Eastern Empire alone and turn his attention to the West. The change demonstrates that Attila was more than a successful barbarian warrior: he, or his advisers (we know he employed Roman secretaries) had a firm grasp of the political rivalries and intrigues in both Eastern and Western Empires in this turbulent period. From his headquarters in the Middle Danube area, he was ideally placed to strike east or west, depending on where he could see opportunities. Attila's old friend and mentor, Aetius, was now, briefly, in control of the Western Empire, based at Ravenna under the titular control of Valentinian III (425–55) who, although vain, spiteful and debauched, was still the successor of Augustus. Aetius now represented imperial authority, rather than being the freelance military leader in Gaul, and as far as Attila was concerned, he became the enemy.

As part of the complex diplomacy of the previous years, Attila had been granted the formal title of *magister militum* (master of the soldiers) or chief of the Western Roman army. This may seem bizarre, given Attila's reputation as the great destroyer of the Empire, but it reflects again the complicated interaction between Romans and barbarians which characterized the period: while barbarians had close links with the Empire and employed Roman civil servants to write Latin letters, many of the 'Roman' soldiers were themselves of Gothic origin and may have spoken no Latin at all. It may be that Attila now wanted to convert his appointment into reality and set himself up in Aetius' place, as chief military supporter of the Empire. It must all have been very confusing to the unfortunate peasants and citizens who were forced to pay for, and provide food for, all these rival armies.

As well as these realpolitik considerations, there was a curious tale of intrigue. To add to the unexpected image of Attila as the consummate politician, we also have Attila as the great lover (at least in the imagination of one lonely Roman princess). The emperor's sister Honoria, who had her own palace at Ravenna, had been rash enough to have an affair with her steward Eugenius. When this was discovered, there was a great scandal, the gossip reaching as far as Constantinople. The unfortunate steward was executed and Honoria forcibly betrothed to an elderly and entirely respectable senator called Herculanus. Honoria, who was clearly a woman of spirit, was not at all pleased with this arrangement. She despatched one of her eunuchs, Hyacinth by name, to Attila with her ring, begging him to come and rescue her from her dreary fate. She may well have imagined herself ruling the Empire as Attila's consort, which raises the intriguing possibility of Attila as Roman emperor. However, being one of Honoria's trusted servants was not a recipe for a long life: Hyacinth was arrested, tortured and made to reveal the plot before he was beheaded. Honoria was handed over to the custody of her doughty mother, Galla Placidia, and is never heard of again. Needless to say, Attila could now assert that he was invading to claim his rightful bride.

A gold coin of the emperor Valentinian III (425–55), whose court was famous for its debauchery. He never took the field himself but his jealousy led him to murder Aetius, the last great soldier of the Roman West. Shortly afterwards he was himself murdered by some of Aetius' followers.

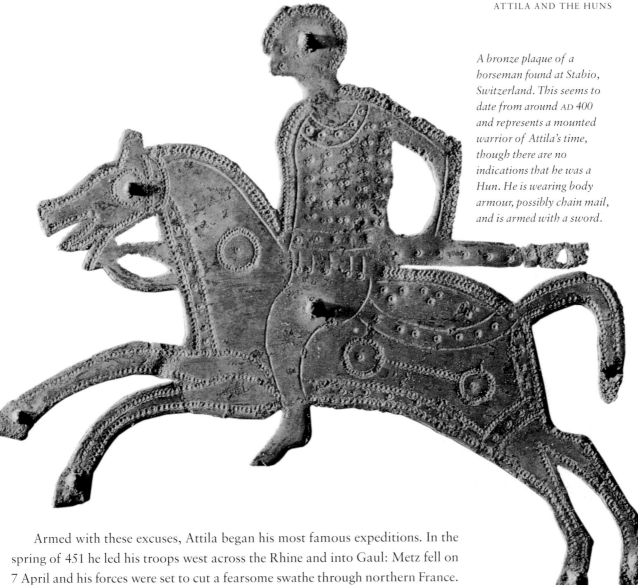

A bronze plaque of a horseman found at Stabio, Switzerland. This seems to date from around AD 400 and represents a mounted warrior of Attila's time, though there are no indications that he was a Hun. He is wearing body armour, possibly chain mail, and is armed with a sword.

Armed with these excuses, Attila began his most famous expeditions. In the spring of 451 he led his troops west across the Rhine and into Gaul: Metz fell on 7 April and his forces were set to cut a fearsome swathe through northern France. In this emergency, Aetius managed to persuade the Visigothic king of Toulouse, Theodoric, who had long been his enemy, to co-operate in the defence of Gaul. When Attila approached Orléans, the allies advanced north to relieve the city. They arrived just in time to prevent it falling to the enemy and Attila was obliged to retreat. He now seems to have lost momentum and been concerned that he might be trapped in Gaul, an unfamiliar country whose agricultural landscapes were unsuitable for the nomad style of warfare.

As he retreated east, Aetius and his men pursued the Huns until they caught up with them in the open country around Châlons-sur-Marne. This open land, the so-called Catalaunian Plains, was the setting for a major battle. On about 20 June the two armies met at a site which cannot now be identified with any precision. From the viewpoint of the military historian the battle is important as it is the only major encounter involving the Huns when led by Attila of which we have any detailed account. Unfortunately our main source, Jordanes, was writing at a later date and does not give a clear outline of events. Attila's army, which probably numbered about 30,000, were not all Huns. There were subject

tribesmen, Gepids and Ostrogoths, whose loyalty and expertise could hardly be entirely relied upon. The 'Roman' army too, included many Visigoths and Alans (another nomad tribe) whose commitment to the cause was equally doubtful. According to Jordanes, 'There was a unyielding and long-drawn-out battle', but that does not tell us very much. Attila fought in the centre of his own line, rather than standing back from the conflict as some later nomad rulers did. It began badly for the Huns when Thorismond, the son of the Gothic king, was able to seize a hill which lay in the middle of the battlefield. What is clear, however, is that Aetius and his Gothic allies fought the Huns to a standstill. By nightfall Attila was forced to take defensive measures and surrounded his camp with wagons to await the next day's assault. It is said that he piled up a heap of saddles, intending to set fire to them and jump into the flames if he was in danger of being taken prisoner. The attack never came. The Visigothic king, Theodoric, had been killed in the conflict and his son, advised by Aetius, left the camp to secure his position in his capital, Toulouse. The probability is that Aetius, who had long been a friend and ally of the Huns, had no wish to see them exterminated and find himself at the mercy of the victorious Visigoths: a balance of power among the barbarians was his main objective.

Attila had saved the bulk of his forces but apparently his experience on the Catalaunian Plains had convinced him that the invasion of Gaul was too risky a project to be worth trying again. Instead, the next year he decided to invade Italy. Taking both

Ruins of the forum at Aquileia. The city was sacked by Attila in his last campaign to Italy in 452. Aquileia, a major regional centre in Roman times, never entirely recovered from the sack and was replaced as the major urban settlement in the area by Venice, which was protected by the waters of the lagoon from barbarian attack.

Aetius and the Roman forces off their guard, he marched from his base on the Danube over the Julian Alps to north-eastern Italy. Here he began to besiege the city of Aquileia, then the most important city of the area. The assault did not prove to be an easy undertaking. Aquileia held out against him and he was on the verge of abandoning the siege as he had done at Orléans the previous year. According to one of those stories which historians feel obliged to repeat because there are no reliable details to recount, Attila saw a stork leaving the city with its young and, knowing how attached these birds were to their homes, he concluded that the situation inside must be desperate and renewed the assault, this time with success. The city was given over to a relentless sack from which it never fully recovered. It was in the aftermath of this and other calamities that the surviving inhabitants sought refuge in the islands of the lagoon that were to develop into the city of Venice. It is a curious thought that without Attila, the Venetian republic might never have been born.

As usual the sack of one city persuaded others to open their doors with alacrity. The cities of northern Italy, including Milan, surrendered and were, in

Pope Leo I confronts Attila and dissuades him from attacking Rome, in this painting by Raphael Sanzio d'Urbina (1483–1520) in the Vatican. Although by this time (452) Attila was on the point of turning back as his army was devastated by disease, the pope's action was celebrated in later centuries in history and art.

the main, able to escape the horrors of a major sack. It was natural that Attila should now turn his attention to Rome. He never made it. Pope Leo I led a delegation to appease him and the embassy persuaded him to retreat north and lead his army back to his homelands. This was not, however, just a triumph of papal diplomacy. The years 451 and 452 were marked by widespread famine: the Huns may have been frugal, but the army had to eat something. More sinister for Attila were the first outbreaks of plague. For centuries, plague did more to protect Italy from northern invasions than any of her armies and Attila was one of the first to suffer. He fully understood that the safety of the Hunnic army was the key to his survival. After the losses of the Catalaunian Plains, he could not risk any further losses. Defeated not by battle but by bacteria, he returned to Hungary, no doubt to decide in which direction to launch an attack the next year.

It was never to be. Attila's death was natural rather than the result of assassination or warfare, but it was in keeping with his flamboyant lifestyle. Attila had many wives, for the custom of the Huns seems to have put no limit on this, but he still wanted new partners. According to the generally accepted story, he married a girl called Ildico who was, as girls always are in these stories, extremely beautiful. On his wedding night he feasted, eating and drinking lavishly before retiring with his new bride. In the morning, his guards were, naturally, reluctant to disturb him. It was not until later in the day that they became concerned about his absence. Eventually they summoned up the courage to break down the door and found the unfortunate Ildico weeping by the body of her blood-covered husband. Apparently he had bled through the nose during his sleep and, being well gone in wine, had suffocated in his own blood.

This fifteenth-century manuscript illustration, from The War of Attila *by Nicola da Casola of the Franco-Italian school, shows Attila and his army on horseback.*

His funeral was spectacular. Horsemen galloped around the body and the Huns commemorated their dead leader with a mixture of wild merriment, desperate grief and copious amounts of alcohol. He was interred in a great barrow, accompanied by a vast quantity of treasure and weapons. Like Genghis Khan's tomb, his resting place has never been found.

There survives, in a Latin version, a garbled translation of the Hunnic song of lament which was composed for the occasion and which shows something of how his people regarded their great chief:

> The Chief of the Huns, King Attila
> Born of his father Mundiuch
> Lord of the bravest tribes.
> More powerful than any before him
> Sole ruler of the kingdoms of the Scythians and Germans
> He terrorized both empires of the Roman world
> Appeased by their prayers
> He took an annual tribute to save their remnants from plunder.
> When he had accomplished all this by the favour of Providence
> Not by an enemy's blow,
> Nor by treachery
> But in the midst of his people at peace
> Happy in his joy
> Without any pain
> He died.
> Who can think of this as death
> When none thinks it calls for vengeance.

It is said that on the very night in which Attila died, the new emperor in Constantinople, Marcian, had a dream in which he saw Attila's bow being broken. Such a dream would certainly have been prophetic. The aftermath of Attila's death clearly demonstrated to what extent the importance of the Huns during this period was of his own creation. It is not clear that Attila was a great general. The one battle we know anything about, the Catalaunian Plains, shows him forced on to the defensive and, in the end, lucky to escape with any of his army intact. If he showed any military talent, it was in knowing when to retreat. He excelled rather as a politician, seeing and seizing the opportunities presented by the weaknesses of the two empires. He offered his men rich new grazing lands, pillage and the gifts of luxury items purchased with the tribute extorted from the settled peoples. Without this sort of leadership, the Huns were unable to keep together. Within a generation of his death, divisions among his successors, and the end of tribute, had scattered and demoralized them. They disappear from the historical record almost entirely, except as a terrible warning of the dangers that these rude nomads could inflict on a sedentary and prosperous society.

CHAPTER TWO

THE ARABS

EARLY ARABIC POETRY AND LEGEND celebrates the lone warrior, with his camel in the desert, defying his enemies and the elements in search of adventure and love. Here a modern Bedouin soldier rides his camel past the crags and peaks of the Wadi Rum in southern Jordan. The early Arab conquerors would have passed this way during their invasion of Syria.

THE ARABS

Nomad warriors have had a dramatic impact on world history on numerous occasions, as we shall see in the rest of this book. On the whole, however, their impact has been destructive and short-lived. The Huns may have precipitated the fall of the Roman Empire in the West, but the successor states which emerged were Romano-Germanic: the Hunnic state disappeared into oblivion and the Hunnic religion never became a force in the spiritual life of western Europe. Similarly, neither Iran nor Russia are today Mongol-speaking countries and, apart perhaps from some scattered remnants along the Volga and in the mountains of northern Afghanistan, there are no populations which seem to have their origins among the Mongol conquerors.

Very different, however, are the consequences of the Arab conquests, from 632 onwards to the Middle East and North Africa. Alone among the nomad warriors, they brought with them a dominant, proselytizing religion, Islam, and this in its train contributed a written language of high culture and, later, of administration: Arabic became not just the language of religion and government, but the spoken vernacular of almost the entire population from the Zagros

Mountains to the Atlantic Ocean. There can be few events which have affected world history so profoundly as the battles and expeditions of the decades between 632 and 720. For better or for worse, we are all living with the consequences at the present day.

The armies of the early Islamic conquests were recruited almost entirely from the Arab populations of the Arabian peninsula and the deserts of Syria and Iraq. In the pre-Islamic period, these populations were linked by language and a certain common culture. Since there was no political organization, the language was a major unifying factor. There were obviously different dialects and the relics of these can be found in the vast numbers of synonyms and alternative meanings that survive in classical Arabic. At the same time, it appears that these differences were no real barrier to communication and that Arabs from the tribes of the Yemen and the Hadramawt in deepest southern Arabia could understand Arabs who tended sheep along the Euphrates Valley and owed allegiance to the Byzantine or Sasanian emperors. Furthermore, in the century or so before the coming of Islam, the Arabs had developed a written form of their language and a common oral culture. The written culture is associated above all with the ancient city of Hira, on the desert frontier of Iraq. Here, on the fringes of the Persian Empire, a semi-independent kingdom had emerged, a sort of buffer state between

Like other nomads, the Arabs lived off their animals. Deep in the deserts of Arabia camels were the only beasts which could survive, but along the fringes of the settled lands in Syria and Iraq most Bedouin lived off their sheep, which they could market in the nearby towns. Though nomads, they were well aware of urban life and the opportunities it offered.

the settled lands and the true desert, ruled by the Arab Lakhmid dynasty. Their court became a magnet for poets and story-tellers from all over the Arabic-speaking areas, serving to spread a common culture. Without these bonds of language and culture, it would have been impossible for the tribes of the Arabian peninsula to work together in the great project of the conquests in the way that they did.

They were also united by a common lifestyle. Most Arabs lived as nomad or semi-nomad tribesmen, in tents, dependent for their subsistence on their animals – either camels, in the inner desert, or sheep, along the margins of the settled lands where both water and markets could be found. They were divided into tribes, each claiming descent from a common ancestor; but apart from this loose framework, they lived in a condition of true anarchy, that is to say, they had no government. Security of life and limb, the most basic service provided by any government, was instead dependent on kin.

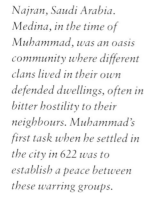

Najran, Saudi Arabia. Medina, in the time of Muhammad, was an oasis community where different clans lived in their own defended dwellings, often in bitter hostility to their neighbours. Muhammad's first task when he settled in the city in 622 was to establish a peace between these warring groups.

Only the threat of vengeance from outraged relatives could secure a man's life and the sanctity of his women and children. In this world, there was no distinction between civilians and the army. As with other nomad societies, every man had to be a potential warrior and avenger.

Tribal identities were important for placing individuals in society, but the large tribe was not the focus for everyday loyalties and protection. Tribes such as the Tamim in north-east Arabia, or the Kinda in the south and centre, had thousands of members scattered in many geographical areas: the tribe seldom, if ever, met as a unit. Instead, most Bedouin lived their lives in much smaller tenting groups, extended families of perhaps a hundred souls, and they often co-operated with people from other tribes. Even among these smaller groups, organization was informal. Authority was concentrated in the hands of leaders, called sharifs in early Arabic, but later known as shaykhs. These figures owed their prestige to their descent; a shaykh had to be from a shaykhly lineage, but within that lineage, it was not the eldest or favourite son who succeeded but the man who could command respect, as leader in war, as finder of grazing and dispenser of

hospitality. The shaykh had no coercive power: a shaykh who demonstrated that he could not deliver would soon find his followers drifting away or choosing another chief. By the same token, a shaykh who proved his skill and intelligence could attract followers from far and wide. This natural selection meant that there was a high standard of competence among military leaders; neither favouritism nor bribery could secure a man loyalty, which could only be based on respect.

Within the smaller tribe, the main movers were the individual Bedouin and their immediate kin. The poetry with which they expressed their values and their culture glorified the individual, the lone horseman, acting on his own initiative, riding through the desert on the camel which might be his only companion, in search of glory, of lost love and the respect of his fellows. No amount of wealth and status could secure the prestige of the warrior or his position in battle. Here,

for example, is the pre-Islamic poet Antara in the late sixth century celebrating his military prowess in a piece of shameless boasting:

I have a high purpose firmer than a rock
And stronger than immovable mountains
And a sword before which the useless spearheads give way
Whenever I strike with it,
And a lance-point which shows me the way
Whenever I lose the path in the night,
And a mettlesome steed behind whom
The lightning trailed from the striking of his hooves.
Dark of hue my horse is, splitting the starless night with blackness
Between its eyes a blaze like the crescent moon.
It would give its own life to save me
And I would ransom it with my life and my fortune on the day of battle.
And whenever the market of the war of the tall lances begins
And blazes with the polished and whetted blades.
I am the chief broker in it
And my spear point is a merchant, buying precious lives
Wild beasts of the wilderness, when war breaks into flame,
Follow me from the empty wastes
Follow me and you will see the blood of the foemen
Streaming between the hillocks and the sands.
Then go back and thank me
And remember what you have seen of my deeds.

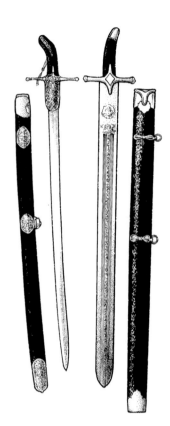

THE SWORDS OF KHALID B. AL-WALID

These swords, currently in the Topkapı Museum in Istanbul, are said to have belonged to Khalid b. al-Walid, the Arab conqueror of Syria, and have been preserved as relics by later generations of Muslims. It is impossible to be sure that they are genuine, but the blades at least may go back to the times of the conquests.

It is the classic image of the loner, with his horse and his arms, his affinity with the wild animals and the desert places, fighting for the honour of his tribe. The spirit of individual heroism and the glorification of the solitary warrior was quite alien to the spirit of steppe nomads such as the Huns and the Mongols, for whom discipline was everything. Of the nomad warriors in this book, only the Vikings celebrated individual prowess in battle in the same way.

And battle was a more or less constant feature of the Bedouin life. There were feuds, caused by murder and vengeance, feuds which could rumble on for generations with sporadic outbursts of violence. These sometimes developed into major military confrontations between large groups, such as the famous war of Basus which divided the tribes around Medina in the last years of the sixth century before the coming of Muhammad. But even if there was no feud, there were constant raids or threats of raids, to round up and drive away the camels or sheep of other tribes. If there were no civilians in this society, neither was there any peace.

The equipment with which these wars were fought was simple but not primitive. The most important item was the sword, a long straight blade with a

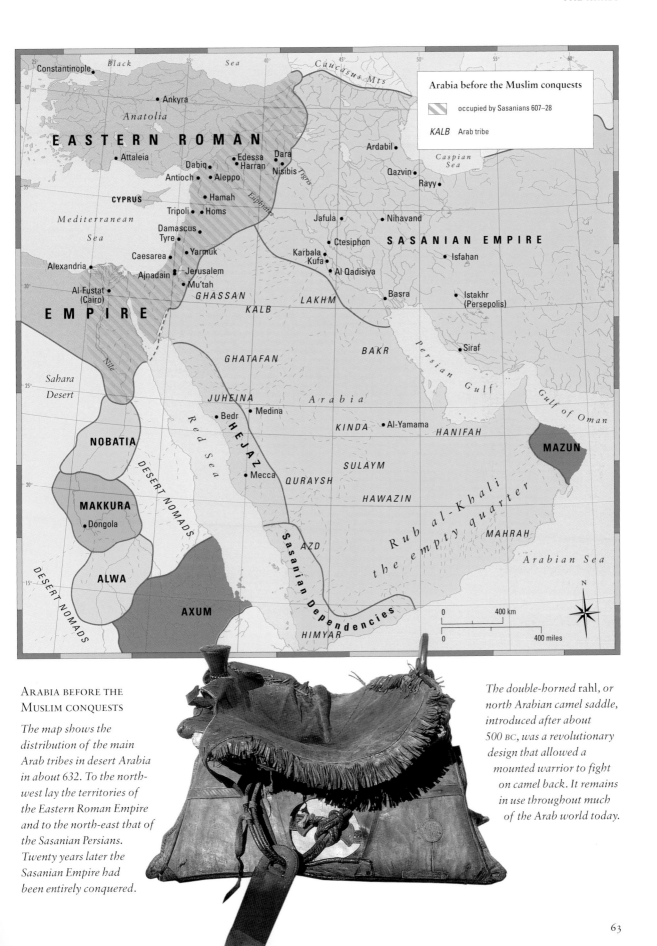

Arabia before the Muslim conquests

occupied by Sasanians 607–28

KALB Arab tribe

Constantinople
Black *Sea*
Ankyra
Anatolia
Caucasus Mts
Ardabil
Caspian Sea

EASTERN ROMAN
Attaleia
Edessa
Dabiq
Harran
Dara
Antioch
Aleppo
Nisibis
Qazvin
Rayy

CYPRUS
Hamah
Euphrates
Jafula
Nihavand

Mediterranean Sea
Tripoli
Homs
Damascus
Tyre
Karbala
Ctesiphon
SASANIAN EMPIRE
Isfahan

Caesarea
Yarmuk
Kufa
Al Qadisiya

Alexandria
Ajnadain
Jerusalem
Basra
Istakhr
(Persepolis)

Al-Fustat
(Cairo)
Mu'tah
GHASSAN

EMPIRE
KALB
LAKHM

Nile
GHATAFAN
BAKR
Persian Gulf
Siraf

Sahara Desert
JUHEINA
Arabia
Gulf of Oman

Bedr
Medina
NOBATIA
HEJAZ
KINDA
Al-Yamama
HANIFAH
MAZUN

MAKKURA
Mecca
QURAYSH
SULAYM
Rub al-Khali the empty quarter
MAHRAH
Dongola
HAWAZIN
Arabian Sea

ALWA
AZD
Sasanian Dependencies

DESERT NOMADS
Red Sea
AXUM
HIMYAR

0   400 km
0   400 miles

N

ARABIA BEFORE THE
MUSLIM CONQUESTS

The map shows the
distribution of the main
Arab tribes in desert Arabia
in about 632. To the north-
west lay the territories of
the Eastern Roman Empire
and to the north-east that of
the Sasanian Persians.
Twenty years later the
Sasanian Empire had
been entirely conquered.

The double-horned rahl, or
north Arabian camel saddle,
introduced after about
500 BC, was a revolutionary
design that allowed a
mounted warrior to fight
on camel back. It remains
in use throughout much
of the Arab world today.

Chain mail largely replaced lamellar armour in the early Muslim period. This, one of the oldest surviving mail-coats in the Arab world, dates from the twelfth century but is very similar to those worn by the early Arab conquerors.

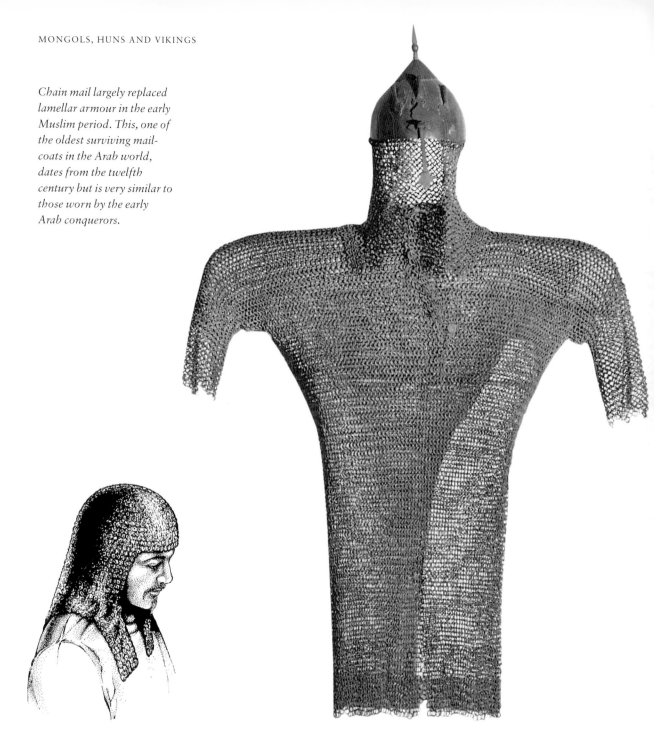

THE *MIGHFAR*

The mighfar *was a sort of mail head covering which also covered the neck and extended down over the shoulders. It could be worn under a metal helmet or on its own. It could also be covered by a turban or simple hood.*

short-handled hilt. Of course the Bedouin did not manufacture these themselves but bought them from the settled communities or had them made by wandering smiths. The steel blades of India and the Yemen were the most highly esteemed, but most warriors must have made do with locally manufactured swords. The spear, too, was an important item. The long, wooden-shafted spear carried a point which was used for piercing but it also had sharpened edges to the point so that it could be used as well for slashing from side to side. Then, too, there was the bow. Unlike the medieval West, where archers normally belonged to inferior social groups compared with the knights, archery enjoyed a high prestige in this early Arab military hierarchy. Great men from famous lineages were pleased to boast of their prowess with the bow in battle. We hear both of Arab bows and Persian bows, but it is not clear what the difference was except that Persian bows may have been longer and heavier. It is evident that these were not the composite bows used by Turkish and Mongol warriors, but rather simple, wooden bows made from the tough, flexible wood of the nab' tree which could be found on the desert margins. Arrows were metal-pointed and feathered. There is no evidence of crossbows. In addition to these formal weapons, the Arabs made use of

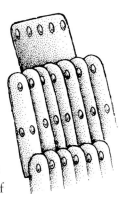

LAMELLAR ARMOUR

Although providing less protection than chain mail, lamellar armour could be made from iron, bronze, whalebone, ivory or horn and needed only a few days to cut and lace together, whereas chain mail needed a skilled armourer, a good supply of iron and several weeks to make.

sticks, stones and anything that came to hand, including tent-poles, which could prove very useful when a camp was being attacked.

The Arabs also made use of defensive armour, or perhaps it would be more accurate to say that some of them did, since the vast majority of tribesmen would have been unable to afford sophisticated body protection. The most common form of armour was chain mail. Development of the use of chain mail, as opposed to lamellar armour (metal plates sewn on to a leather or fabric coat) seems to have occurred in the Roman armies of late antiquity and it must have been from them, or from the Sasanians, that the Arabs acquired it. There are no surviving suits of mail from an Arab context before the twelfth century, but from

This painting of an Arab hunter comes from the desert palace of Qasr al-Hayr West (Syria) built in about AD 720. As he is dressed for the hunt rather than for battle, he wears no armour. In contrast to the warriors of the Hunnic period, he is clearly using stirrups, a fairly recent invention at this time.

The armies of Sasanian Iran used heavy cavalry as a mainstay of their forces. On this silver plate, probably of the sixth century, a Sasanian king is shown hunting lions with a bow. Both rider and horse are richly caparisoned and he carries the long straight sword characteristic of the period.

descriptions in the sources they seem to have covered the body, not the leg, often being worn under a linen outer garment. One form of head protection was the metal helmet known in Arabic as a *bayda*, i.e. an egg from its rounded shape, generally without a nose-piece. It is not clear how common these helmets were and many men must have fought in turbans or other sorts of fabric headdresses. More characteristic was the *mighfar*. This was essentially an aventail – a piece of mail to protect the back of the neck. The Arab *mighfar* also covered the top of the head and could be worn over a helmet or as a head-covering on its own. Armour, like metal weapons was expensive. It was privately owned and would be passed down from generation to generation in the same family.

There can be no doubt that Arab society on the eve of the great conquests

was highly militarized, in the sense that a large proportion of the adult male population (and some of the women) possessed weapons and were competent in their use. However, this society lacked any form of central direction. Apart from occasional raids on settled areas, such as the one which led to the Arab victory over the Sasanians at Dhu Qar in 610, the military energies of the Arabs were largely directed at their fellow Arabs from other tribes or groups. Until the early seventh century, this population had never united against an outside enemy and its overall military potential was largely untried. The coming of Islam changed all this.

The Prophet Muhammad did not come from a Bedouin background, although he certainly knew the Bedouin well from his early youth. He was born

Unlike the oasis town of Medina with its gardens and palm groves, Mecca, seen here in a nineteenth-century engraving, is in a narrow valley surrounded by barren mountains. It survived through trade and the reputation of its pagan shrine, which was developed into the Muslim Kaaba after Muhammad's conquest of the city in 630.

and brought up among the merchant aristocracy of Mecca, a city which had risen to prominence as the major commercial centre in Arabia in the second half of the sixth century. The Quraysh tribe from whom he sprang stood apart from the tribal rivalries of the time because of their guardianship of the prestigious pagan cult centre at Mecca and the trading alliances they forged at the fairs held under the protection of the shrine. When in 622 Muhammad fled from Mecca to the oasis settlement of Medina, some two hundred miles to the north, he became effective leader of a small state. In some ways the early Muslims resembled a newly created tribe whose members looked after and protected one another and waged war against their rivals, notably the merchant aristocracy of Mecca. However, Muhammad was much more than a Bedouin shaykh; he was the Prophet of Allah and his leadership was based not just on consent, but on divine authority as well. As more and more tribes in Arabia, and finally the Meccans themselves, accepted his authority, he made it clear that warfare between Muslim tribes was not permitted: disputes were to be solved by his arbitration and the judgement of God.

On the Prophet's death in 632 many of the tribes of Arabia had accepted his leadership. Immediately, however, with the breaking of what most regarded as a personal bond, they began to drift away. This might easily have marked the end of the story of Islam, with the Arab conquests remembered merely as one of history's more improbable 'might-have-beens', but for the decisive action taken by the early Muslim leadership, notably by the first two caliphs (or successors of the Prophet) Abu Bakr (632–4) and 'Umar (634–44). Like Muhammad himself, they were from urban commercial backgrounds, but they saw clearly that the Muslim community had to expand or break up. Unless they could direct the military energies of the Arabs against outside enemies, Muslim tribes would start to fight against one another and community and religion alike would vanish. It was this change of direction which motivated the great Arab conquests.

We have a great deal of literary information about the Arab conquests – too much in some ways – but it does not always create a coherent picture. The stories of the victorious campaigns were not written down immediately. Rather they were memorized and recounted as tales by the participants, and later by the sons and grandsons of the participants. No doubt the tales lost nothing in the retelling. By the time these accounts came to be written down in their existing form in the mid and late eighth century, much embellishment had occurred. They had been perpetrated by men who wished to preserve the memory of their own ancestors' achievements rather than provide a chronicle record and if these achievements needed imaginative enhancement, then so be it. Furthermore, the activities of the early Muslims and the decisions of the caliphs became normative; men wanting to make a point about eighth-century politics would dress up their polemic as the history of the early days of Islam. So, while we have a mass of information, it is often difficult to separate truth from fancy. In some cases we cannot be sure of the dates of the major battles, let alone the course of the conflict and the reasons for the Arab success. Nor are Byzantine or other outside sources much help. Apart from some fragments, the main Byzantine narrative of the Arab conquests, that of the monk Theophanes, is ultimately derived from Arab accounts and is not that of an independent witness.

Despite these limitations, we can be reasonably certain about the general outlines. The Muslim assault on Syria had begun even before Muhammad's death. In 629 a small Muslim army raided to the borderlands of the Byzantine Empire to the east of the Dead Sea in what is now southern Jordan. It was not a

A shady path in an Arabian oasis. Although most of the warriors who made up the Arab armies came from nomad tribes, the leaders, including Muhammad and the early caliphs who succeeded him, came from urban or village backgrounds.

success: the Muslim army of perhaps 3,000 men was met by a Byzantine force and decisively defeated. Its commander, Muhammad's adopted son Zayd, was killed and the remnants of the army had to be salvaged by Khalid b. al-Walid, later to become the most famous of Arab generals.

After the Prophet's death, the first priority of the leadership was to reduce by force of arms those Arabs who had broken away from the Muslim community. This was done swiftly and brutally, but whereas rival leaders, such as the 'false' prophet Musaylima, were not spared, most of the Arab tribesmen were simply recruited into Muslim armies and directed against the Iraqi frontiers of the Sasanian empire. Like the later Mongol armies, these of the early Muslims increased in size as the conquests progressed, sweeping up other Arabs and later, Persians and Berbers into their ranks. Soon afterwards, the conquest of Iraq and Syria began. Both these lands were, or had been, prosperous farming countries supporting large cities and markets. In terms of population, wealth and administrative organization, they were vastly superior to anything which could have been found in Arabia. Their people enjoyed a much higher standard of living than the lizard-eating Bedouin. However, a century or so previously the Muslim conquests had undermined this prosperous stability. In 541 bubonic plague (Black

The invading Arabs found Syria full of cities. Many, like Apamea, shown here, still retained their great classical buildings but the cities had suffered badly from plague, earthquakes and Persian invasions, and the days of their greatest prosperity were long past.

Death) struck and it returned with merciless severity throughout the century. We cannot know the extent of the mortality but if comparisons between the Black Death of 1348–9 in western Europe are anything to go by, then the population loss may have been anything up to a third of the entire population. Furthermore, the diseases would have created maximum havoc among the people of the densely populated cities and villages where rats (the great carriers of the plague) could thrive. In contrast the open, Spartan environment of the Bedouin encampment would probably have kept infection at bay.

A more immediate catastrophe was the series of wars between the Byzantines and the Persians. The two great empires of antiquity had always fought along

their common borders in northern Syria and Mesopotamia. For centuries this war had been a match more or less of equals and the frontier had remained stable with only minor adjustments. The early seventh century saw all that change. After 602 the Sasanian Shah Khusraw II launched a devastating assault, the Byzantine armies collapsed and all the rich provinces of Syria, Palestine and Egypt fell into the hands of the invaders. Byzantine armies were destroyed and the Byzantine administration collapsed. However, the Persians were unable to

The Arab conquerors of Iraq were amazed by the wealth and splendour of the Sasanian royal palaces. The great arch of the palace at Ctesiphon, near Baghdad, still survives to give an idea of the scale of the building. Arab soldiers picnicked in the great halls and cut up the jewelled carpets to sell in the market place.

conquer Constantinople itself and the remnants of the Roman Empire proved unexpectedly resilient. The emperor Heraclius (610–41) launched a great counter-attack. With immense strategic daring he led his army along the Black Sea behind the Persian lines and struck at the soft underbelly of the Sasanian Empire in Iraq. In 628 the Persian capital at Ctesiphon fell, the discredited Khusraw was deposed and murdered and the True Cross returned in triumph to Jerusalem.

The war may have resulted in victory for Heraclius, but both sides had suffered grievously, their armies and economies lay in ruins, their administrative systems were shattered. It was against this background that the Muslims achieved their astonishing successes.

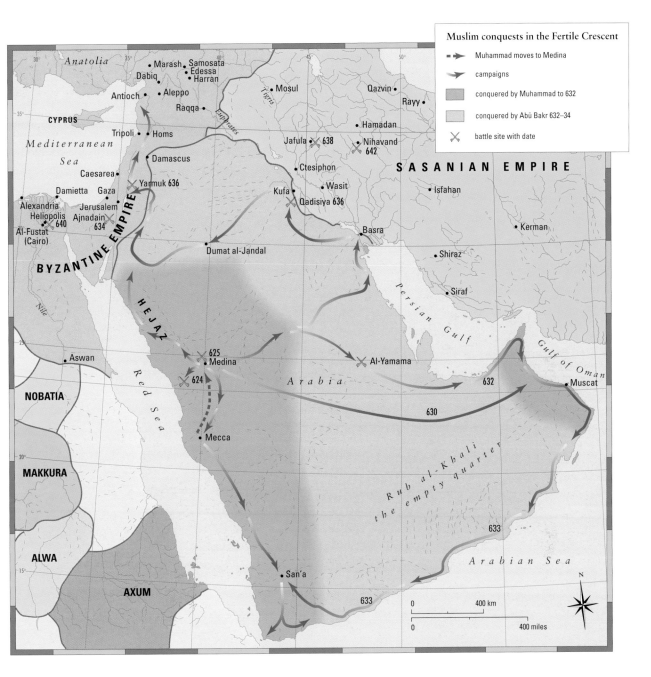

Muslim conquests in the Fertile Crescent

➡ Muhammad moves to Medina

➤ campaigns

☐ conquered by Muhammad to 632

☐ conquered by Abū Bakr 632–34

✕ battle site with date

The conquest of Iraq began as a continuation of the campaigns against the dissident Arab tribes of north-eastern Arabia. When, by the end of 633, these had been forced to accept the authority of Medina, the Muslim force, commanded by Khalid b. al-Walid, naturally moved to subdue the Arab populations of frontier towns such as Hira. But the Arabs were in for a nasty shock. Around 634 the Muslim army suffered a sharp defeat at the battle of the Bridge, probably near where the city of Kufa was later founded. The commander Abu 'Ubayd (Khalid had by this time been transferred to the Syrian front) was killed. The remnants of the army retreated into the desert, a safe haven where the Sasanians with their slower, more heavily equipped forces, would not dare to penetrate. A lesser

MUSLIM CONQUESTS IN THE FERTILE CRESCENT

The map shows the movements of Muslim armies after Muhammad's migration to Medina in 622. The early battles of Badr and Uhud were fought against the Meccans. After the conquest of Mecca in 630, armies were sent to southern Arabia and the Syrian and Iraqi borderlands.

commander than 'Umar might have taken this defeat as a sign that the Muslim conquest had already reached its natural frontier but instead he recruited a new and larger army, including many tribesmen who had broken away from the Muslim community after Muhammad's death, and sent them to Iraq under the command of one of the Prophet's companions, Sa'd b. Abi Waqqas. Once again the Persian army mobilized and came out to meet the Muslims at a place called Qadisiya, not far from the site of the previous encounter. The battle was probably fought in 636. Despite the fact that the Persian army was much larger than the Arab, this time the results were very different. For reasons which the narrative sources do not make clear, the Persian army was decisively defeated. It may be that the intrigues that followed the deposition and death of Khusraw II had left the high command seriously divided. It may also be that the Persians made a mistake in advancing into the desert around Qadisiya rather than awaiting the Arabs in the populated areas where their opponents would be on unfamiliar territory. For whatever reason, the Persians were decisively defeated and most of their army fled, although a number of élite troops chose to defect to the Muslims and join the army of conquest.

The whole of Iraq, the breadbasket of the Sasanian Empire, now lay open. Arabic sources delight in telling how the simple (but, of course, pious and God-guided) Bedouin pillaged the great Sasanian palace at Ctesiphon, cutting up the jewelled carpets and ransacking the great storehouses. News of such success travels fast, and Arabs from the desert who had hung back were now eager to join the advancing armies.

Meanwhile Arab armies had also been making progress on the Syrian front. The course of events here seems to have been more complex than in Iraq and this may explain why there are a larger number of differing accounts. Apparently 633 saw little more than minor encounters with frontier garrisons. This changed with the arrival, probably in 634, of Khalid b. al-Walid from the Iraqi front. Khalid's journey from one theatre of war to the other has aroused great interest among military historians because he seems to have moved his troops rapidly across a terrain of waterless desert generally believed to be impassable, and so surprised his enemies. As with so many events during this period, there are conflicting accounts. According to one version, he made his way up the Euphrates and along the old caravan route which led through Palmyra to Syria. This is a sensible route and it may have been the one he travelled, but early accounts all agree that his forces encountered great problems with thirst. It is said that they had to go six entirely waterless days and did not have enough skins to carry supplies. To solve this problem Khalid ordered that camels should be forced to drink great quantities of water and their mouths were bound to prevent them from chewing the cud. They were subsequently used as animated water-tankers, slaughtered as required and the water drunk from their stomachs. This may not sound very appetizing, but faced with the alternative of dying from thirst, the Muslim troops must have suppressed any queasiness they may have felt. The six-day march is

The invading Arab armies had to march through the rugged landscapes of southern Jordan, a land of ravines, gullies and small villages perched on the tops of the hills. Such landscapes can still be seen today, as here at the village of Dana looking west towards the Dead Sea.

said to have taken place between two wells whose names are given but which cannot now be identified with any certainty.

This story may be no more than a traditional tale which has been attached to Khalid's name, but if true it can hardly have happened on the Palmyra route which is, by the standards of the Syrian desert, comparatively well watered. If we accept this, then it seems likely that Khalid may have travelled by the southern, alternative route through Dumat al-Jandal, a remote oasis lying about half-way between southern Iraq and Jordan. To lead an army by this route would be an extraordinary feat of daring. There are no other records of armies ever coming this way for the very good reason that it was waterless for long stretches. Even if Khalid's force were no more than 500 to 800 strong, the most likely estimate, the feat still indicates a military leader of genius. It was the kind of long-range

A view of the Yarmuk river valley on the Jordan–Syria border. It was in this rugged territory just to the north of the river that Arab and Byzantine armies met in 636. The defeat at the Yarmuk marked the effective end of Byzantine power in Syria and opened the way to the Arab conquerors.

outflanking operation which Subedei was to perfect at the time of the Mongol conquests five hundred years later.

The story of Khalid's desert crossing is proof that the Muslims were able to use the desert to achieve mobility and surprise, and gain an advantage denied to their opponents. It also shows how the command in Medina could assert effective control over the conduct of field operations and order commanders around as and when it deemed necessary.

The numbers in Khalid's force may have been small, but their arrival seems to have transformed the position in Syria from a sideshow to a major field of conflict. According to one account, he surprised and routed the Christian Arabs of the Ghassanid tribe, the Byzantines' main allies in the area, as they were celebrating Easter, probably in 634. This surprise concentrated the mind of the Byzantine Emperor Heraclius on the threat that the Arabs now posed. This threat became more ominous as they began to take possession of cities along the desert margin such as Bostra and possibly Damascus, where many of the population were themselves already Arabic-speaking and may have been sympathetic to the invaders. Local Byzantine forces were defeated in battles at Ajnadayn and Pella in the Jordan valley.

Heraclius then gathered the largest army he had at his disposal, including many tough Armenian troops from the Caucasus area, and sent them to confront the Muslim armies at the River Yarmuk, on the present Jordanian-Syrian border. The battle of Yarmuk, which probably took place in August 636, is the only battle in the course of the Arab conquests where the sources enable us to reconstruct the conflict in any detail, although even here there are contradictions and confusions. It is also the only battle for which the site can be identified with any precision, the rocky landscape and deep wadis, as well as the remains of the Roman bridge, allowing us to plot the movements of the armies. The Muslim army may have numbered 20,000 men while the Byzantine forces were probably somewhat larger,

even though Muslim accounts tend to talk up their numbers and represent the Arabs as fighting against enormous odds. Even before the battle, there seem to have been tensions among the Byzantine commanders and between the Byzantine army and the local inhabitants of the area, most of whom were Arabs even if they were not Muslims. It may be that the army had supply problems as a result.

At the start of the battle, the Byzantine forces advanced to Jabiya, the summer camping grounds of their Ghassanid allies. As the Muslims fell back, they moved up into the area between the wadis of Ruqqad and Allan, and their line may have become over-extended. It seems that the Muslim right tempted the Byzantine left wing to advance by feigning flight and that the Muslim cavalry managed to outflank the Byzantines. Khalid then drove a wedge between the Byzantine cavalry and infantry. A key tactical objective was achieved when the Muslims captured the only bridge across the Wadi'l Ruqqad, effectively cutting off the Byzantine retreat. It was at this point that Byzantine resistance began to crumble. Rumours were spread that the Ghassanids and their followers had fled. Uncertainty turned to panic and many Byzantine soldiers attempted to escape down the steep banks of the wadis and were driven to their deaths. A dust storm sprang up (it was high summer) obscuring much of the action, and the Byzantine army was largely destroyed.

The story of the battle of Yarmuk reveals much about the nature of Arab military success. Both in tactics and strategy, the Arabs were surprisingly conventional. There were no great tactical ideas, none of the overwhelming mustering of forces and movements of encirclement which characterized Mongol victories. There were no secret weapons. The Muslims drew up a battle line, with left wing, right wing and centre, just as their enemies did. An Arab general at the end of the seventh century described the progress of battle to his inexperienced troops before they encountered the enemy in the following words: 'The first stage of fighting is the shooting of arrows, then the pointing of spears, then

THE BATTLE OF YARMUK 636

The battle of Yarmuk in 636 was the decisive event which opened Syria to the Arab armies. The Byzantines, operating in unfamiliar terrain, were outmanoeuvred and their troops were driven down the rocky ravines to the river where many perished. After this defeat, the emperor Heraclius abandoned Syria and withdrew beyond the Taurus mountains.

① Initial Byzantine attacks

② Muslim advance

BYZANTINES

Jabiya

Nawa

Fiq

Wadi'l Allan

Dayr Ayyub

Yaqusa

①

②

Wadi'l Ruqqad

Wadi'l Yarmuk

MUSLIMS

Golan Heights

Fiq

Wadi'l Ruqqad

Yaqusa

Wadi'l Yarmuk

⑤

The battle of Yarmuk
AD 636

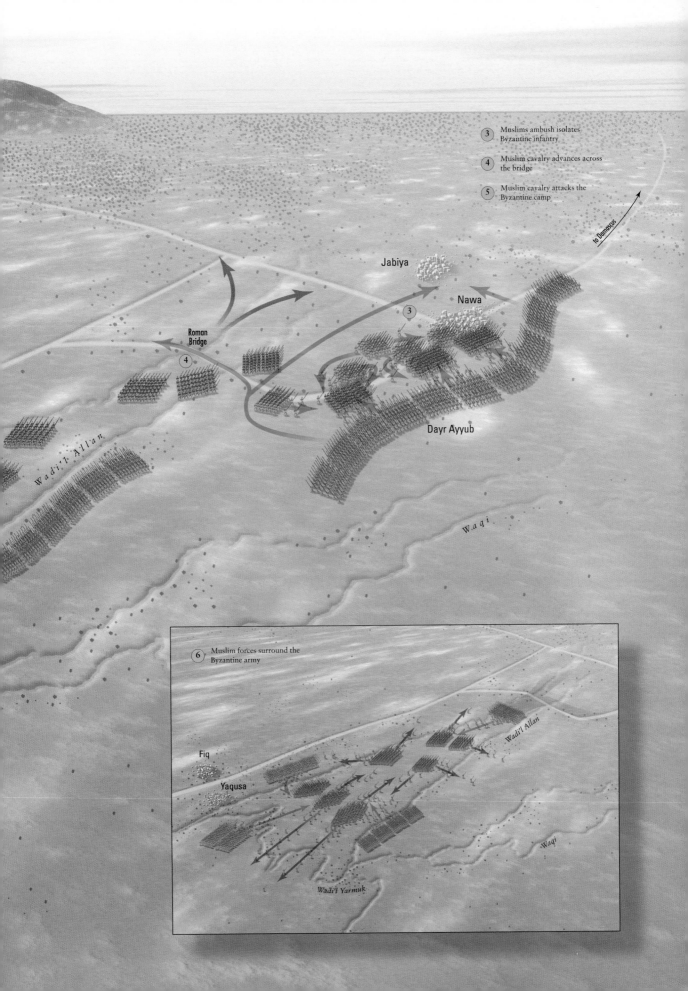

3   Muslims ambush isolates
     Byzantine infantry

4   Muslim cavalry advances across
     the bridge

5   Muslim cavalry attacks the
     Byzantine camp

to Damascus

Jabiya

Nawa

Roman
Bridge

4

Wadi'l Allan

Dayr Ayyub

3

Waqi

6   Muslim forces surround the
     Byzantine army

Fiq

Yaqusa

Wadi'l Allan

Waqi

Wadi'l Yarmuk

The Nile valley. In 641 a small Arab force, led by 'Amr b. al-'As, invaded Egypt and captured the Byzantine fortress at Babylon (Old Cairo) and the city of Alexandria. The rest of Egypt rapidly came under their rule in the years that followed and Egypt became an Arabic-speaking Muslim country.

the thrusting of them to the left and right and finally the drawing of swords. That's all there is to it.' The Muslims may also have been more familiar with the landscape, though there is no evidence for this, and they may have been given help by local sympathizers, but again there is no proof. They simply fought a conventional battle and fought it better and more effectively than their enemies.

Just as the battle of Qadisiya laid open the rich lands of Iraq, so the defeat of the Byzantines at the Yarmuk enabled the Arabs to take control of Syria. The redoubtable Emperor Heraclius, veteran of so many triumphs and disasters, retired beyond the Taurus mountains lamenting that he was leaving so sweet a land to his enemies. The towns and cities of Syria and Palestine were left to fend for themselves and few resisted for long. Antioch, the political capital, and holy Jerusalem had both fallen by the end of 638. Only Caesarea on the coast, which could be supplied from the sea, held out, probably until 641.

The conquests of Iraq and Syria were only the beginning of the extraordinary story of Arab expansion. In the east, the Persian forces were defeated again at

Nihavand which left the Iranian plateau open to the Muslim advance. The last Sasanian shah, fleeing with his entourage, was pursued all the way to distant Merv, a garrison fortress on the north-eastern frontier of his empire. Here in 650 or 651 he was killed, not by the advancing Arabs but by a local miller who coveted his finery.

In the west too, the Muslim advance continued. The conquest of Egypt was virtually a private enterprise operation, led in 641 by a Meccan aristocrat called 'Amr b. al-'As. After the fall of Syria, Amr gathered a force, certainly no more than 15,000 strong, and set off for Egypt. The Byzantine administration was hopelessly divided and was extremely unpopular with many of the local Coptic Christians, who had been persecuted as heretics by the Byzantine authorities. 'Amr took the massive Roman fortress, confusingly known as Babylon, just to the south of where modern Cairo stands, and this allowed him a stranglehold on the country. As in Syria, it was only the port city of Alexandria which held out for any length of time, finally capitulating in 641.

There were other conquests to come. Raids all along the North African coast,

In the west, the Arab expansion continued through North Africa to Spain, which was taken in the series of lightning campaigns between 711 and 716. Spain soon became the centre of a vibrant Muslim culture, traces of which can still be seen on the mosque of Cordoba, the earliest sections of which date from the late eighth century.

through the Maghreb to the Atlantic Ocean and eventually, in 711 to Spain. In the east Muslim armies doggedly reduced the cities beyond the Oxus – Bukhara and Samarkand – to obedience. Even more audacious and far-flung were the expeditions of 711–12 when Muslim armies penetrated the wild deserts of southern Afghanistan to take over the rich cities of the Indus valley and establish the province of Sind.

To understand the success of Muslim arms, some common preconceptions need to be discarded. For a start, Muslim armies were just that – armies, not migrations of tribes or peoples. The armies which defeated the Sasanians and Byzantines were composed of adult males bringing with them their military equipment, such as it was, but not their families and flocks. The migrations followed later.

Nor were the Muslim armies 'tribal' in their organization. It is true that men from the same tribe tended to fight together. Tribal banners and war cries were important rallying points and illustrations of some of the early tribal banners have been passed down in old texts. However, they were also subject to a degree of military discipline. We are told that at the time of the battle of Qadisiya, the Muslim general Saʻd b. Abi Waqqas established a system of divisions of the army into decimal units each commanded by an *ʻarif* or junior officer. However, this

In the north-eastern provinces of the Sasanian Empire the Arabs conquered the great trading cities of the Silk Routes, including Bukhara and Samarkand. They made their main base at Merv (Turkmenistan). The round citadel, seen here, was first constructed in around 500 BC and was still in use when the Arabs arrived in AD 650.

picture of neatly formed units may well be the result of projecting later systems back to the early days rather than reflecting a precocious organization.

One feature which did mark the Muslim armies out from their opponents was their degree of mobility. The retreat of the Arab forces into the desert after the disastrous battle of the Bridge and the expeditions of Khalid b. al-Walid show how this mobility afforded them the advantages of both surprise and sanctuary which their opponents lacked. To achieve this mobility the Arab armies were equipped with horses and camels. This did not mean that they were a cavalry army in the style of the knights of western Europe from the eleventh century or of the Mongol horse archers. Generally, the animals carried the soldiers to the battlefield, but serious fighting was done on foot. There is no record of horse archery from the time of the nomad warfare before Islam or the Arab conquests. This preference for fighting on foot was partly, no doubt, because they had no stirrups. There is still uncertainty about the chronology of the appearance of the stirrup but it seems clear that Muslim armies did not adopt the device until after the year 700 when we find mention of them in accounts of warfare in Iran. How important the stirrup was in the development of cavalry warfare is uncertain: after all, the fact that Greeks, Romans and Persians alike had effective cavalry forces without stirrups shows that they were not essential. Yet the fact that they

By 720 the full extent of the Arab conquests is apparent. Egypt and North Africa have been taken, Spain has been occupied and raids are being launched deep into France. In 732 the Arabs are defeated by Charles Martel at the battle of Poitiers, ending their expansion into western Europe. Only the Byzantine Empire offers serious resistance to the conquerors.

The great mud-brick walls and towers still surround the old city at Merv. Originally founded by the Achaemenian kings of Iran, the city was extended by the successors of Alexander the Great and was an outpost of the Sasanians against the Turkish nomads of Central Asia. It remained a major urban centre until it was sacked by the Mongols in 1221.

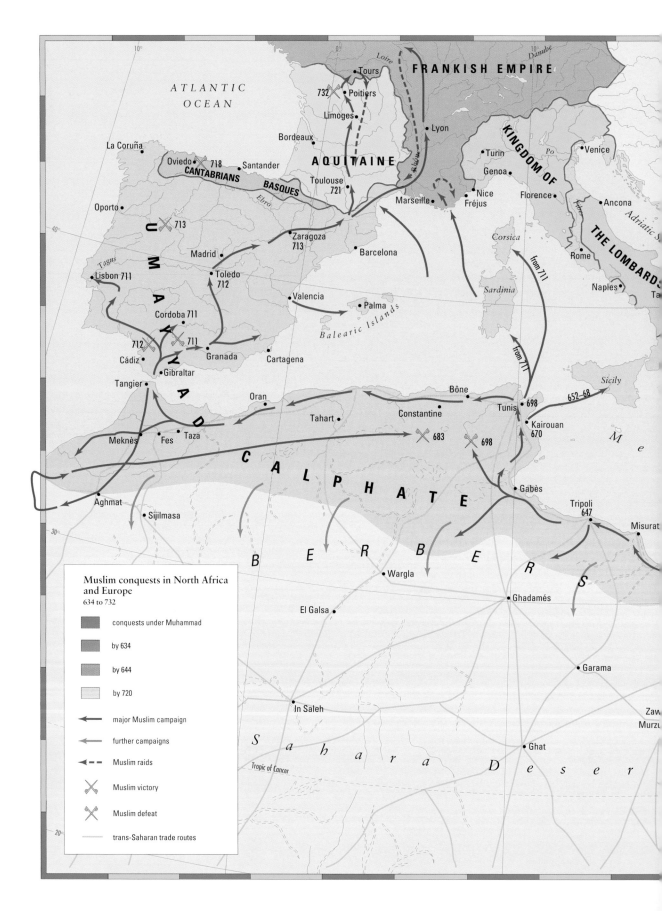

ATLANTIC
OCEAN

FRANKISH EMPIRE

732 Tours
Poitiers
Limoges
Lyon
Bordeaux
La Coruña
KINGDOM OF
Turin
Venice
Oviedo **718**
Santander
CANTABRIANS
BASQUES
AQUITAINE
Genoa
Po
Toulouse
721
Ebro
Florence
Ancona
Oporto
713
Madrid
Zaragoza
713
Barcelona
Nice
Fréjus
Marseille
THE LOMBARDS
Rome
Corsica
Tagus
Toledo
712
Lisbon **711**
Valencia
Palma
Balearic Islands
Sardinia
Naples
Cordoba **711**
712
711
Granada
Cartagena
Cádiz
Gibraltar
from 711
Sicily
Tangier
Oran
Bône
Tunis **698**
652–68
Meknès
Fes
Taza
Tahart
Constantine
Kairouan
670
M
e
Aghmat
Sijilmasa
Wargla
CALIPHATE
683
698
Gabès
Tripoli
647
Misurat
Ghadamés
Garama
El Galsa
Ghat
In Saleh
Zaw
Murzu
Sahara
Desert
Tropic of Cancer
from 711
UMAYYAD
BERBERS

Muslim conquests in North Africa and Europe
634 to 732

- conquests under Muhammad
- by 634
- by 644
- by 720
- major Muslim campaign
- further campaigns
- Muslim raids
- Muslim victory
- Muslim defeat
- trans-Saharan trade routes

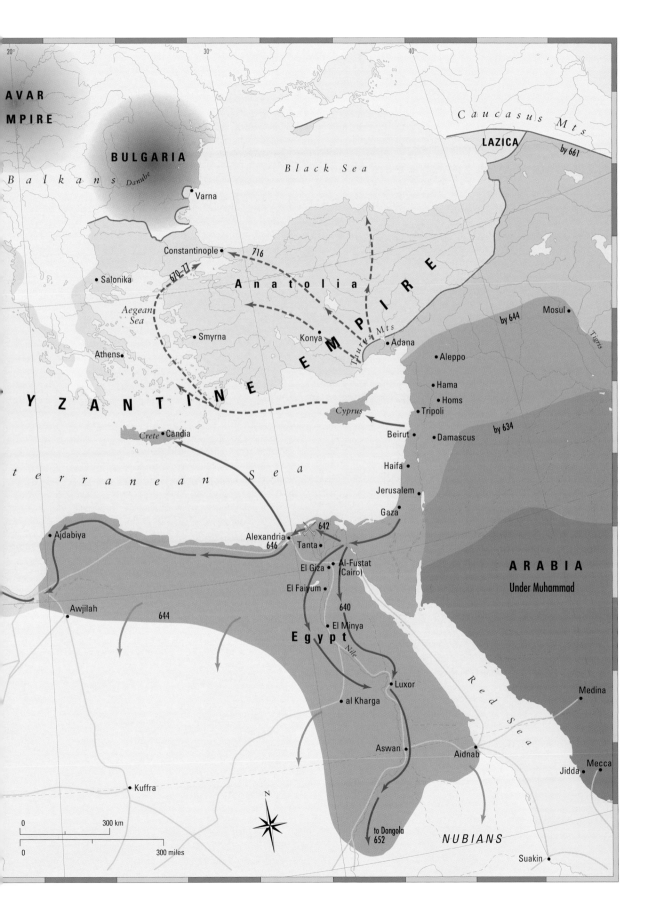

AVAR
MPIRE

BULGARIA

Black Sea

Balkans *Danube*

• Varna

Caucasus Mts

LAZICA

by 661

Constantinople • 716

670-77

• Salonika

A n a t o l i a

by 644

Mosul •

*Aegean
Sea*

• Smyrna

Konya •

Taurus Mts

• Adana

Aleppo •

• Hama

Tigris

Athens•

B Y Z A N T I N E   E M P I R E

• Homs

• Tripoli

Beirut • • Damascus

by 634

Cyprus

Crete • Candia

Haifa •

by 634

A R A B I A

terranean   Sea

Jerusalem •

Gaza •

ARABIA

Under Muhammad

• Ajdabiya

642

Alexandria •
646   Tanta •

El Giza • • Al-Fustat
(Cairo)

El Faiyum •

640

Awjilah •

644

• El Minya

E g y p t

Nile

• Luxor

Medina •

• al Kharga

Aswan •   Aidnab •

Red   Sea

• Kuffra

Mecca •

Jidda •

0   300 km

0   300 miles

N

to Dongola
652

NUBIANS

Suakin •

MUSLIM CONQUESTS IN IRAN AND THE EAST

The eastern expansion of the Arabs rapidly took them to the borders of China and India. Iran was largely conquered by 651. The push into Central Asia was harder and slower and the people of the mountains of Afghanistan offered stubborn resistance. In 751 a Muslim army defeated the Chinese at Talas, the furthest point of Arab expansion in the east.

spread so fast throughout the Middle East, the Byzantine world and Europe suggests that they offered obvious advantages in cavalry warfare.

In Arab warfare of the late seventh and eighth centuries, when the armies had become settled in garrison cities, they seem to have perfected a sort of wall of spears technique. An army faced by advancing horsemen would dismount, kneel in line with the ends of their spears in the ground behind them and the points directed at the enemy. Here they would remain until the enemy was almost upon them and only then would they rise or thrust their spears at the nostrils of the enemy horses. This technique was effective time and again but, of course, it needed training, discipline and considerable nerve to keep the line in the face of a wild and formidable attacking force. In fact, all the reports we have of this tactic are from accounts of inter-Muslim civil wars and there is no record of it being used at the time of the Muslim conquests or among the Bedouin tribes, where heroic action and individual prowess were very much to the forefront.

Another tactic, which may have been borrowed from Roman military practice was the construction of a *khandaq*. The word *khandaq* comes from the Persian word for a trench, and as used by early Muslim armies it was a ditch and rampart made of earth and stones. This had first been employed by the Prophet Muhammad himself in 626 when the Meccan forces attacked his stronghold of Medina. He ordered the digging of such a ditch on the vulnerable side of the city and the Meccan cavalry were unable to penetrate it. With such a distinguished example to follow, Muslim commanders frequently used the *khandaq* to protect their men, especially when they were facing Bedouin brigands in the years following the conquests. In the hands of an experienced commander, the *khandaq* could become a real marching camp, with four walls enclosing an area in which the army could pitch their tents, and gates in each of the sides. As in accounts of Roman warfare, prudent

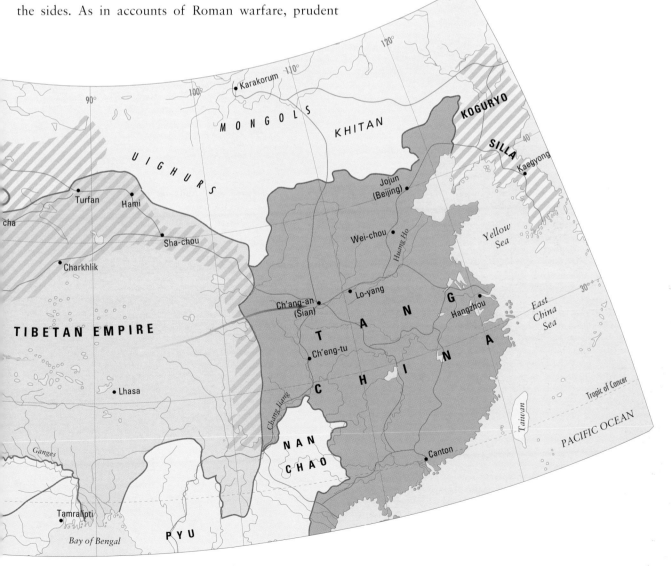

commanders took care to build their camps and post sentries; rash or vainglorious leaders failed to do so and disaster resulted.

As might be expected, the Arab armies had little experience or competence in siege warfare. The Greek historian Procopius, writing in the sixth century, noted how even a simple wall would deter the 'Saracens'. It is logical to wonder, then, why the great fortified cities of the Byzantine and Sasanian Empires were unable to resist the nomad invaders. After all, cities like Antioch and Damascus in Syria had Roman fortifications which have survived in part down to the twenty-first century. We have very little information about sieges during the Muslim conquests. When the Arab armies were attacking Damascus, they are said to have borrowed ladders from a neighbouring monastery to scale the walls, which hardly sounds like highly developed siege warfare.

The early Muslims never seem to have used the torsion artillery which had been developed by the Romans (that is, basically, artillery in which the power is generated by twisted ropes or sinews). From an early stage, however, they did know the use of the swing-beam siege engine, later known in the West as the trebuchet. This is essentially a long beam mounted on a stand or pivot which allows both ends to go up or down. The beam is mounted such that the pivot is much nearer one end of the beam than the other. At the end of the 'long' end there is a sling and the ammunition (usually stone balls) is placed in it. At the other 'short' end of the beam ropes are attached. When the order is given, men pull sharply down on the ropes, the 'long' end swings swiftly up and the sling flies

In contrast to the great mud-brick walls of Central Asia, the Arabs in Syria were confronted with the stone walls and towers of the Roman fortifications, seen here at Sergiopolis (Rusafa) and (insert) at Apamea. Despite the strength of these defences, most cities surrendered peacefully after the defeat of the Byzantine field army at Yarmuk in 636.

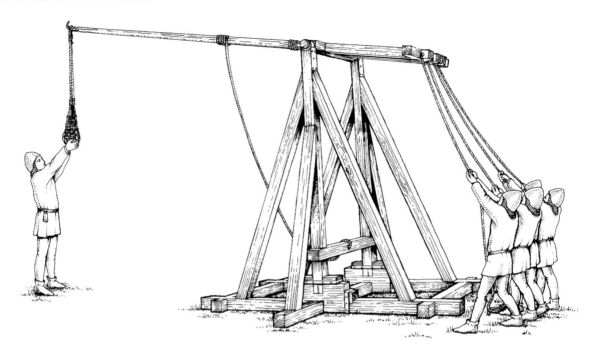

A TRACTION TREBUCHET

Compared with the Romans, the early Arab armies only had comparatively simple siege engines. However, they did make use of the swing-beam trebuchet. This originally came from China and is first recorded in the West in the late sixth century. This is a hand-powered traction trebuchet. It was not until the twelfth century that the more powerful counterweight trebuchet came into use.

round the end to deliver the projectile with considerable force. This device seems to have been both simpler and more effective than the artillery of the classical period and soon replaced it entirely. The device first appears in the West at the time of the siege of Thessalonika by the Avars (a nomad people from Central Asia) in 597. The early Muslim armies certainly knew of it but their machines seem to have been too small to be effective against fortifications. Instead they appear to have been used as anti-personnel weapons, placed outside walls or mounted by defenders on the wall-head. We also hear of them being used as a sort of field artillery on the open battlefield.

In 691 the ruthless governor al-Hajjaj was besieging rebels against the Umayyad caliphs, who had taken refuge in the sacred Kaaba in Mecca itself. Arabic historians describe in fascinated horror how he used a trebuchet to hurl bricks and stones at the sacred structure. This seems to be the first record we have of Muslim armies using engines against buildings. These early versions were all traction trebuchets, i.e. men on ropes provided the motive power. By the thirteenth century, a new form, the counterweight trebuchet in which the power was generated by the fall of a heavy sand-box, was in common use. It was the counterweight trebuchet which formed the highly effective artillery used by the Mongols and their Mameluke contemporaries. There are also a number of accounts, from Shushtar in south-west Iran for example, of how treachery among the inhabitants enabled the Muslims to penetrate the walls of fortified cities. In none of the accounts, however, do we hear of siege engines being used or of walls being undermined. Whereas the Mongol conquerors were to employ or cajole large numbers of Chinese and Persian sappers and artillery men into working for them, there is no record of this happening in the Arab conquests.

The explanation for the success of the Arabs in taking fortified cities is probably more psychological than military. The campaigns of the Arab conquests were won and lost in the great field battles, notably at Qadisiya and Yarmuk. With the destruction of the Sasanian and Byzantine armies and the retreat and death of the monarchs, it was clear that no one was going to come to the rescue. But there was another side to this. Submitting to the Arab conquerors was comparatively painless. There were none of the large-scale massacres which characterized Hunnic or Mongol conquests of cities. The invaders did not expel the inhabitants or seize all their property. Still less did they force the people to convert to Islam, for non-Muslims paid higher taxes than the faithful. It is true that they demanded tribute and it is also true that some members of the Greek-speaking élites of Syria and Palestine chose to flee to the West. And if they demanded taxes, what was new in that? Byzantine and Persian rulers had certainly extorted taxes which may well have been higher. Anyway, many people may have deluded themselves that the Arabs would soon be gone: better pay them off than risk destruction or death. These psychological factors were as important in the Arab conquests as systematic terror was in those of the Mongols.

Apart from mobility, the strategic advantages of the Arab nomads over the settled and more technologically advanced enemies lay in their experience and their morale. There are a number of stories in the Muslim sources about how their enemies, Byzantine or Sasanian, chained their soldiers together to prevent them running away from the battlefield. There are other tales from both Muslim and non-Muslim backgrounds about the rivalries of their enemies' commanders or tensions between the armies and those they were ostensibly trying to protect. We should not take the account of the chains literally; even the most unintelligent commander must have realized that this was unlikely to improve battlefield performance, but the stories may be making a real point about the nature of conscript or impressed armies. Similarly, the stories of tensions may not be true in their details but point to a general malaise and loss of morale.

In contrast, the Muslim forces enjoyed high morale. For many of them this was a religious commitment; no doubt many believed that they were doing Allah's will and that he would support them. At crucial moments, too, they may have felt certain that death in battle would be martyrdom and lead directly to the joys of paradise so vividly described in the Quran. There were also older motivating forces: love of booty for example. Byzantine and Sasanian soldiers were not likely to pick up much from their ragged Bedouin opponents, whereas for the Arabs, all the glittering prizes of civilization lay before them. Tribal solidarity, or more accurately the *esprit de corps* that is generated among small groups of men who eat, sleep, travel and fight together, must also have played its part: gathered around their banners with men they had known from birth and who may have been relations, they would not have wished to show fear. Many would have been stimulated by the image of the lone warrior, the hero whose reputation would live forever among his tribe. Self-confidence and individual self-reliance surely inspired men far from home and family to press forward into ever stranger and more remote territories in search of plunder, adventure and fame.

CHAPTER THREE

THE ARRIVAL OF THE TURKS

THE TURKISH MERCENARY SOLDIERS *employed by the ʿAbbasid caliphs in the ninth century were housed in the garrison city of Samarra, about a hundred miles north of Baghdad, to minimize conflict with the local people. The walls of the Great Mosque of the mid ninth century clearly show the military nature of the city.*

THE ARRIVAL OF THE TURKS

THE MUSLIM EMPIRE was created by one group of nomad warriors, the Arabs, but in the military sphere, it came to be dominated by another, the Turks. In modern usage the term Turks is used to described the inhabitants of the republic of Turkey, the vast majority of whom are, of course, settled townspeople and farmers. In the longer sweep of history, however, the term is used to describe a very different people, or group of peoples.

Like the Huns, the Turks originated in the vast steppe lands and grass plains which lie between Russia and Iran in the west and China in the east. In the south these lands are bordered by the Gobi Desert and the Takla Makan, in the north by the Siberian forests. The climate is characterized by hot summers and ferociously cold winters. These lands have always been the home of nomad populations, since the land is not fertile enough, and the climate not temperate enough, to encourage permanent settlement.

The Turks appear quite suddenly on the stage of world history. In 552, in circumstances which are now obscure the Turks replaced a mysterious people called the Juan-Juan as rulers of the steppe lands. Where they came from is uncertain, though the early Turks may have been connected with iron mining and smelting in the area. The ruler of this power took the title of Kaghan which, in various forms (Khan, Qa'an, Khaqan, etc.) was to be the generic title of rulers of Central Asia down to the beginning of the twentieth century. In the late sixth century this new power established diplomatic relations with the Byzantine Empire in an effort to bypass Iran and break the Sasanian stranglehold over the silk trade.

Despite divisions and fierce tribal rivalries, the Turkish Empire survived until 745. As with Arabic among the Bedouin, an element of unity was provided by a common language which enabled people from all parts of the vast empire to understand one another. The language, and some of the history of these early Turks, is recorded in a remarkable series of inscriptions found in the valley of the Orkhon river, now in northern Mongolia. They also seem to have had common religious ceremonies, including human sacrifice at funerals, and probably a common lifestyle. The Turkish Empire may only have lasted for a couple of centuries, but it brought the Turks to the notice of the world and from then on the peoples of Inner Asia and their language were generally known as Turks and Turkish.

The Arab conquerors of eastern Iran had come into conflict with the hardy Turks of Central Asia. With the breakup of the Turkish Empire, Turks began to be recruited as professional soldiers in the armies of the caliphs, ultimately displacing both Arabs and Iranians as the military élite. It was their quality as nomad warriors which made them so valuable to rulers. In the mid ninth century, when the Turks were a comparatively new military force, the Arab essayist and

A Central Asian warrior of the eighth to tenth century. This bust clearly shows the eastern Asiatic features which Arab and Persian commentators noted as typical of the Turkish soldiers employed by the caliphs.

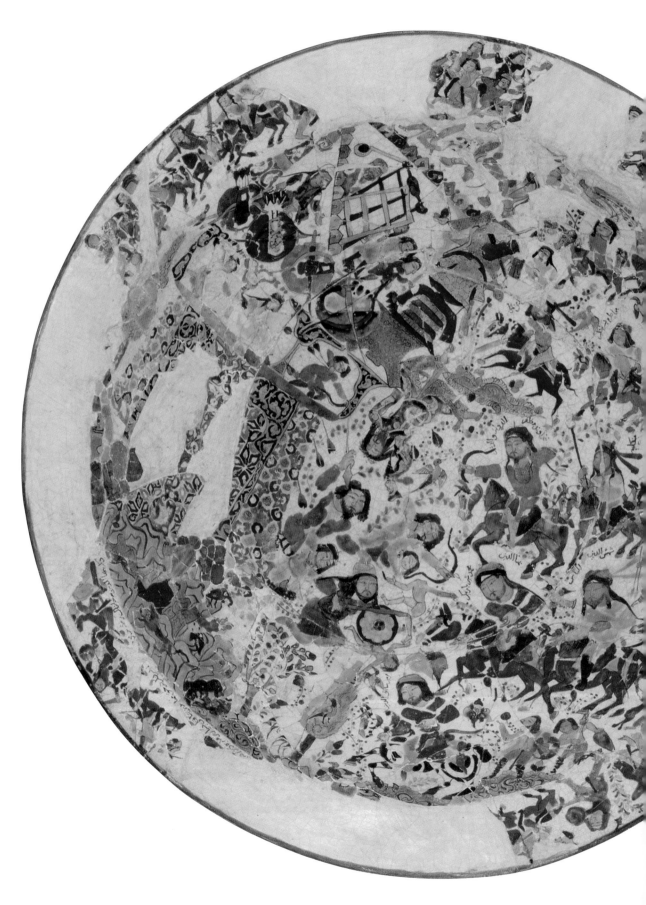

commentator, al-Jahiz (d. 868), produced a short treatise on 'The Excellences of the Turks' in which he describes a discussion about their particular virtues as warriors. This is worth quoting at some length because it provides a contemporary, eye-witness explanation as to why these nomad warriors were so highly valued as fighting men.

One of the features which al-Jahiz notes is their physical endurance:

Turkish warriors in action, from an early thirteenth-century plate. Here a castle (lower left) is being besieged by an army of horsemen, each armed with spear and bow. Note the catapult mounted on the castle as a defensive weapon.

> When a Turk travels with a non-Turkish army he travels twenty miles for the ten other people do. He cuts off from the army to right or left, racing to the summits of peaks or penetrating the bottoms of valleys in search of game. At the same time, he shoots at everything which creeps, steps, flies and lands. When a journey lasts a long time, travel becomes hard, the camp site is far away and midday is reached, then fatigue becomes intense. People are overcome with weariness, they grow silent and do not speak because their preoccupation with their own hardships keeps them from conversation. Everything wilts from the intensity of the heat or perishes from numbing cold. Even the strongest traveller longs for the earth to swallow him up. When he sees a horseman or spots a flag, he is cheered up by that and is happy in the thought that he has reached the camp site. When the rider eventually arrives, he dismounts and walks bow-legged like a boy needing to urinate. He groans like a sick man, yawns, stretches and lies down. At this time you see the Turk, who has already travelled twice as far as anyone else and whose shoulders are weary from pulling the bow, galloping after a wild ass, gazelle, fox or hare.

Al-Jahiz records the observation of a colleague on the behaviour of the army of the caliph al-Ma'mun (813–33), at a time when Turks were beginning to be recruited for the caliphs' armies:

> On one of the campaigns of al-Ma'mun I saw two ranks of horses on both sides of the road near the camp, a hundred Turkish cavalrymen on one side of the road and a hundred non-Turks on the other. They had been lining up to await the arrival of the Caliph. It was past midday and the heat was intense. While all except three or four of the Turks were still sitting on their horses, all except three or four of the non-Turks had dismounted and were lying on the ground.

The relationship between the Turk and his horse was remarkable:

The Turk is more skilled than the veterinarian and better at teaching his mount what he wants than the most skilled trainer. He bred it and raised it as a foal. It followed him when he called and galloped behind him when he galloped ... if you sum up the life of a Turk, you will find he sits longer on the back of his mount than on the surface of the earth. When the Turk rides a stallion or mare and sets off on a raid or a hunting trip, the mare and her foals follow him. If he is unable to hunt people, he hunts wild animals. If he is unsuccessful in that, or needs food, he bleeds one of his horses. If thirsty, he milks one of his mares, if he wants to rest the one he is riding, he mounts another without touching the ground. There is no one else whose body would not rebel against a diet comprised entirely of meat. His mount, on the other hand, is satisfied with stubble, grass and shrubs. He does not shade it from the sun or cover it against the cold.

Of course it was their prowess in battle that attracted most attention. One of the participants in the discussion contrasts the Turks with the Kharijites (Arab Bedouin rebels against the caliphs):

If a thousand Turkish horsemen attack, they shoot a single volley, felling a thousand horsemen. What would remain of any army after this sort of attack? The Kharijites and the Bedouin are not known for shooting from horseback. The Turk shoots at wild animals and birds, at the *birjas* (a target on a spear), people or any other target. He shoots while his mount is galloping backwards and forwards, right and left, up and down. he shoots ten arrows before the Kharijite can notch a single one ... his lasso is unbelievable, the way it reaches the horse and seizes the rider in one throw ... They taught horsemen to carry two or three bows and a corresponding number of strings ... the spear of the Kharijite is long and solid, the spear of the Turk is short and hollow. Short, hollow spears are more penetrating and lighter to carry.

With this toughness and military ability, went a certain sort of amorality. One observer noted:

We can see that the Turk does not fight for religion or dogma, or to acquire political control or the land-tax, or because of group spirit, for zeal for the sacred and sacrosanct, out of anger or enmity for his fatherland or to protect house and wealth. He only fights for plunder. He makes his own choices. He does not fear divine retribution if he flees or hope for divine favour if he fights bravely [unlike the Muslim warrior in the *jihad* or holy war].

The picture al-Jahiz presents is precise and familiar from the much more sketchy accounts we have of the Huns. These themes were to be taken up by later commentators on the Mongols. The Turks were remarkable for their hardiness, their relationship with their horses (which were not just mounts but a source of emergency supplies, so dispensing with cumbersome baggage trains) and their skill as mounted archers as well as with the short spear and the lasso.

From the mid ninth century, these hardy nomad warriors were valued troops of Muslim rulers throughout the Middle East. Many of them were purchased as slaves from the Central Asia or the steppes north of the Black Sea and the Caucasus. But these were no ordinary slaves, powerless chattels to be ordered around. From an early date, these slave soldiers, often known as mamelukes (which simply means slave or owned man) began to acquire power and influence. In the Ghaznevid kingdom which flourished in the area now known as Afghanistan at the end of the tenth and the beginning of the eleventh century, we hear of a regular system of education and promotion of these nomad recruits. According to the great Seljuk vizier, Nizam al-Mulk, writing in the 1080s, the system worked like this:

After a young man [the word used is *ghulam*, another word for slave soldier] was bought he was obliged to serve for one year on foot at a rider's stirrup ... and during this year he was not allowed to ride a horse in private or in public. If he did so and was found out, he was punished.

An aerial view of the garrison city of Samarra, built in the ninth century. The compounds laid out for the Turkish generals and their soldiers can clearly be seen. In the foreground is the wide main street with one of the mosques centre left. In the top right the River Tigris, the only source of water for the city, can just be glimpsed.

After a year the tent-leader spoke to the chamberlain on his behalf and he was given a small Turkish horse with a saddle in untanned leather and a plain bridge and stirrup leathers. After serving for two years with a horse and whip, in his third year he was given a belt to gird on his waist [perhaps with the implication that he now carried a sword]. In the fourth year he was given a quiver and a bow-case [and presumably a bow] which he put on when he mounted. In his fifth year he got a better saddle and bridle with stars on it, together with a handsome cloak and a mace which he hung on the mace ring ... In the eighth year they gave him a single-apex, sixteen-peg tent and put three newly purchased young soldiers in his troop. They gave him the title of tent-leader and dressed him in a black felt hat decorated with silver wire and a cloak made at Ganja [a town in the Caucasus].

This plate from the early thirteenth century shows the mounted Turkish archer at work. The mounted archer, like the armoured knight in Western European warfare, was the élite soldier of the medieval Middle East. Like the knight, he needed specialist equipment and training.

A horse bit from Central Asia, tenth century. The Turks prided themselves on being able to make all their own military equipment rather than depending on city-based craftsmen. This meant that their armies were self-sufficient and highly mobile.

Eventually, the writer goes on, he might be an Amir and governor of a province.

The account is certainly idealized and it was most unlikely to have been as systematic as Nizam al-Mulk claimed: he was after all, presenting a model to his master, the Seljuk sultan Malik Shah (1072–92), rather than writing objective history. It does show, however, how a young man from a Turkish nomad background could be brought up and groomed to be both a military leader and an urbane court functionary. All such boys, it is implied, started from the same point. As chattel slaves, they had no tribal or family connections and promotion was based on merit and talent. It was indeed a real meritocracy in which advancement depended on ability and hard work.

There was another side to the employment of these Turkish boys. With their round moon faces and black hair and eyebrows, many sultans and amirs found them sexually desirable. The cruel beauty of the slave boy, whose eyebrows were like bows and whose eyes flashed like arrows, was a key image in the emergent Persian love poetry of the era. In this complicated world, such a Turkish boy might at one and the same time be his owner's slave, his soldier, his bedfellow and, in the game of love, his cruel master.

All these Turks entered the Muslim world as individual slaves. From around 1040 however, a new pattern began to emerge. At about this time Ghuzz Turks of the area to the east of the Aral Sea (modern Kazakhstan), led by the Seljuk family began to migrate westward en masse, women, children, flocks and all, in search of grazing. They were impoverished and desperate and asked only for space. The then Ghaznevid sultan dismissed their entreaties with contempt and they were virtually forced to confront his army. At Dandanqan, near Merv in Turkmenistan in 1040, this ragged band of nomads defeated the largest and most effective army in the Middle East. Now the defences were down, they swept on through Iran, taking Baghdad in 1055.

The year 1040 marks the point at which the settled governments of the Middle East lost control to the Turkish nomads on their borders. From this point until the consolidation of the Safavid Empire in the sixteenth century, nomad warriors dominated the political life of the eastern Islamic world. It was, in a real sense, the heyday of the nomad warrior.

The strengths of nomad armies were demonstrated once again at the battle of Manzikert on 24 August, 1071 when the Seljuk nomads under the command of the sultan Alp Arslan (1063–72) – 'Hero Lion', a wonderfully evocative name – defeated the Byzantine army led by the emperor Romanus IV Diogenes (1067–71) in eastern Turkey to the north of Lake Van. Unlike many battles of the period, we have full descriptions of what happened at Manzikert, notably an eye-witness account by a Byzantine official, Michael Attaleiates, travelling with the army. Thus we can see more clearly than usual how a nomad force, though probably smaller and certainly less well equipped than their opponents, could none the less humiliate them in battle.

The background of the conflict was the Byzantine attempt to protect the high plateau of central and eastern Anatolia against the incursions of Turkish nomads. The heartlands of the Byzantine Empire lay far to the west, in the towns and villages around the Aegean Sea and, of course, the great city of Constantinople itself. Eastern Anatolia was far away and a very different environment. The population was sparse, the harvests meagre and the cities little more than castles with dependent villages. For the Byzantines this was difficult terrain in which to maintain and supply an army. For the Turks, on the other hand, the high grasslands were not dissimilar to the Central Asian homelands; they could raid these areas almost at will. The fortresses were able to hold out but the countryside in between was slipping inexorably out of Byzantine control.

The emperor Romanus was an experienced soldier. Like many generals before and since faced by an elusive and fast-moving enemy, he believed that if he could bring them to a pitched battle, they could be destroyed once and for all. In the summer of 1071 he led the Byzantine army east. It is impossible to be certain

about the numbers, but the imperial army may have numbered around 40,000. Like many Byzantine armies of the period, this was a polyglot force. There were Greek-speaking soldiers from the themes (military provinces) of Anatolia but there were also Armenians from eastern Anatolia itself, Norman and German mercenaries who had come east attracted by the good wages the Byzantines could offer, and groups of Turks, serving under contract with the imperial forces. Communication between these groups must have been difficult and suspicions of disloyalty and cowardice easily stirred up in times of stress.

A large proportion of the army were foot-soldiers. As they marched east through the increasingly bare landscapes, they were ordered to collect rations for two months. It was harvest time and food could be found (though no one of course gave any thought as to how the local peasants were going to survive the next winter after the army had devoured their supplies). According to Attaleiates, the Byzantine army advanced with 1,000 wagons and 10,000 head of cattle: movement must have been very slow.

A Byzantine army pursues a fleeing band of Muslim soldiers, from an eleventh-century Byzantine manuscript. The Muslims seem to be more lightly armoured but in many ways their equipment is strikingly similar (at least as noted by this artist).

The shores of Lake Van near Akhlat. As the Byzantine armies advanced east in 1071 to confront the Seljuks they found themselves in an exposed situation with very long lines of communication from their bases in the west. These rugged landscapes suited the hardy Turkish horsemen perfectly.

The battle of Manzikert
August 1071

1 24 August: foraging units attacked by the Turks

2 Bryennios' troops attempt to chase raiders but are forced to withdraw

3 Basilakes' cavalry is ambushed and many are captured

4 The remaining troops flee to Manzikert

5 Bryennios and his entire left-wing division attempt to drive off the Turks, but are forced to withdraw

6 25 August: the Turks attempt to seize the riverbank behind the imperial camp but are driven off

7 Initial Byzantine advance: Turks attack and withdraw, harrying Byzantine forces with archery

Phase 1

Phase 2

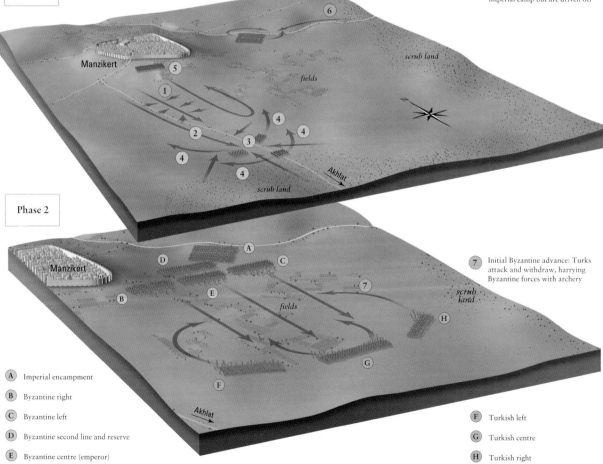

A Imperial encampment

B Byzantine right

C Byzantine left

D Byzantine second line and reserve

E Byzantine centre (emperor)

F Turkish left

G Turkish centre

H Turkish right

Predictably, the response of the Turks was to make themselves scarce. The tribesmen who had infiltrated Anatolia would hardly have dared to risk a confrontation but Alp Arslan wanted to secure his north-western flank so that he could lead an assault on Egypt, his main objective. Negotiations for a truce broke down and the sultan prepared for an armed confrontation.

Meanwhile, the Byzantines moved ever further east with the intention of taking two fortresses, Akhlat on the shores of Lake Van and Manzikert which had fallen to the Turks. These would have provided bases for Byzantine forces in the area but the emperor's real motive may have been to provoke the Turks into a pitched battle.

It was at this stage that the weaknesses of the Byzantine position became apparent. The most important failure was in intelligence. The Turks, who were familiar with the country and moved swiftly through it, certainly knew all about the movements of the Byzantine army. The Byzantines, on the other hand, were very much in the dark. Romanus had no idea that Alp Arslan was leading an

THE BATTLE OF MANZIKERT 1071

Manzikert was a classic example of the triumph of the mobile nomad warriors over a better equipped but slower army. The Byzantines were lured away from the safety of the walls of the city by a feigned retreat and then encircled and destroyed. But treachery in Byzantine ranks also played a part.

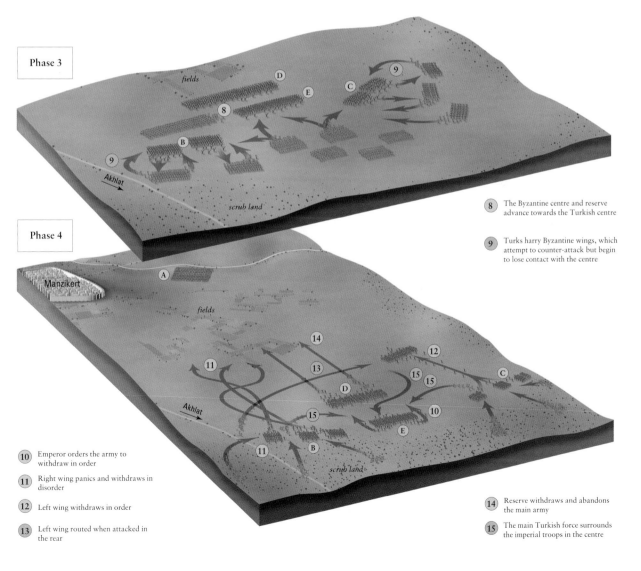

Phase 3

Phase 4

8 The Byzantine centre and reserve advance towards the Turkish centre

9 Turks harry Byzantine wings, which attempt to counter-attack but begin to lose contact with the centre

10 Emperor orders the army to withdraw in order

11 Right wing panics and withdraws in disorder

12 Left wing withdraws in order

13 Left wing routed when attacked in the rear

14 Reserve withdraws and abandons the main army

15 The main Turkish force surrounds the imperial troops in the centre

army to oppose him and imagined that the sultan was far away in Iraq trying to raise troops and that the Byzantine army would only be confronting groups of nomad tribesmen. Faced by what he believed to be scattered and ill-disciplined brigands, he began dividing his army up, some to take Akhlat, others to remain with him at Manzikert.

The town of Manzikert was taken almost immediately and the Byzantines camped outside the city walls. They soon began to meet groups of Turks. On the morning after the fall of the town, the Byzantine left wing, whilst foraging for supplies, encountered some Turks, who immediately took flight. On the assumption that they were dealing with a small group of nomads, the Byzantine commander made a fatal mistake: going against established military practice, he allowed his men to set off in pursuit. The feigned retreat was a classic nomad tactic but it still caught their enemies by surprise. The left wing soon found itself ambushed in rough terrain: many were cut down and the survivors told the emperor that he was facing a much larger and more organized army than he had imagined.

It was clear that there was going to be a major battle. On the morning of 26 August, the Byzantine forces began to advance south from the city. The army was drawn up in the traditional way, the left and right wings with the emperor, and much of the heavy cavalry in the centre. A key element was the rearguard, who were kept well back from the main forces to secure the retreat: if the army had to withdraw at any stage, they would prevent encirclement. The Seljuk army was less formally arranged. The troops were spread out in a extended crescent and while there was a left and right wing, the men probably fought in smaller and more mobile groups. In contrast to the emperor, the sultan kept back from the main line of battle where he could see what was going on and, just as important, he could be seen by his men.

All the Turks seem to have been horsemen and most of them were probably mounted archers. There is no mention of Seljuk foot soldiers. The emperor knew that he had to close with the enemy as soon as possible; the Turks, for the same reasons, knew that they should avoid close encounters and aim to encircle the enemy, raining arrows on them until they were finally exhausted. The Turkish centre retreated, luring the Byzantine centre forward, while on either side the mounted archers harassed the Byzantine wings, forcing them to move much more slowly as they struggled to defend themselves against the deadly hail of arrows. Every so often, groups of Byzantine soldiers, provoked beyond endurance, would attempt to pursue their tormentors. This of course was just what the Turks wanted and they enticed the soldiers away from the main army before turning on them and destroying them.

As the day wore on, Romanus knew that he was in trouble: he had failed to close with the enemy and was losing contact with his wings. He therefore did the sensible thing, and ordered a retreat so that the army could move back to the protection of the walls of Manzikert and regroup. Even in the most ideal of circumstances, an organized withdrawal is an extremely difficult manoeuvre. All pre-modern armies faced difficult problems of communication on the battlefield and, with Turkish horsemen galloping in and out between the units, communication broke down almost completely. Many soldiers on the flanks believed that the emperor had fallen and that the battle was lost. They began to break and flee.

It was at this time that the rearguard should have played their part, protecting the retreat and stemming the panic. But the commander of the rearguard was a sworn enemy of the emperor who could not resist the opportunity of seeing him humiliated. In an action that everyone saw as treachery, he simply ordered his troops to march away and leave the army to its fate. By nightfall, the bulk of the Byzantine forces had been surrounded and many had been killed. The emperor himself was taken prisoner and led before Alp Arslan, who treated him with dignity and respect and released him shortly afterwards. The Byzantine army had lost a battle though it had not yet lost the war. However, the emperor was discredited and was soon done to death by his Byzantine rivals and the army divided into different groups and factions. Meanwhile, the Turks entered Anatolia in ever increasing numbers and Turkey was well on its way to being Turkish.

The success of the Seljuk nomads was based above all on their mobility. Unburdened by a supply train, or by slow-moving infantry, they could outmanoeuvre their opponents at every moment, retreating or closing in as they wanted. This mobility also meant that they had much better intelligence: and whereas their scouts were well aware of the size and progress of the Byzantine army, the Byzantines, in both the run-up to the encounter and in the course of the battle, were often acting in confusion and incomprehension. The mounted archers were the killing force. The relentless cloud of arrows was almost impossible to withstand for any length of time. It was not until the development of effective firearms that the armies of the settled peoples had an adequate response to the nomad advantage in firepower.

Long, straight swords of Sasanian origin (sixth or seventh century). Swords of this type and shape remained common in Middle Eastern armies down to the time of the Mongol conquests when shorter, curved swords became more usual.

—·⫶·◦ɘ◖◦◗◦⫶·—

GENGHIS KHAN
AND THE MONGOLS

GENGHIS KHAN (c. 1170–1227) out falconing, from a
Chinese silk painting. This pastoral, almost intimate
view of Genghis stands in contrast to his ferocious
reputation in other sources. Genghis' grandson Kubilai
Khan became accepted as emperor of China and the
Chinese image of the family was not always hostile.

GENGHIS KHAN AND THE MONGOLS

O F ALL THE NOMAD PEOPLES who emerged from the great steppes of Inner Asia to attack the settled peoples on their borders, none have left such a fearsome reputation as the Mongols. This is partly because of their undoubted ferocity but also because we know so much more about them. Persian and Chinese chroniclers, some of them working as bureaucrats in the service of Mongol rulers, give us vivid accounts of the Mongol conquests. Interestingly, authors such as Juvayni and Rashid al-Din did not see the need to tone down their accounts of Mongol cruelties at all: their patrons could be expected to revel in the ferocity of their ancestors.

We also have a number of accounts by western travellers who visited the Mongol court after the conquests were over; indeed, the Mongols with their strange customs and obvious 'otherness', may be said to have inspired the first ethnographic writing in the western European tradition. The most famous of these travellers was, of course, Marco Polo although some have cast doubts as to whether he really did travel as widely as he claims. Earlier travellers, notably William of Rubruck and John of Piano Carpini visited the Mongols in the generation after the great conquests when many of the primitive Mongol customs still survived.

We also have numerous contemporary illustrations of Mongol and Turco-Mongol warriors. At the beginning of the fourteenth century, Rashid al-Din's chronicle was illustrated by a whole series of drawings of warriors in action. Admittedly, most of the ostensible subjects of these illustrations are pre-Mongol rulers but there can be no doubt that they reflect the details of contemporary

The siege of a city as shown in an early fourteenth-century Persian manuscript. Here we see a counterweight trebuchet in action. Note the complex wooden framework to provide stability and the winch for winding down the long arm. The development of the counterweight trebuchet in the twelfth century meant that artillery could destroy major stone fortifications.

military equipment and siege warfare. At the other end of the Mongol world, there are Japanese paintings celebrating the resistance of Japan to the Mongol forces of Kubilai Khan. Throughout the fourteenth and fifteenth centuries, Persian painters, too, continued to depict, in loving detail, the activities of warriors and hunters. Many of these illustrations are highly sanitized; costumes are refined and radiant with primary colours, but the particulars of military equipment seem to ring true.

The Mongols were closely related to the Turks in custom and language. In the twelfth century they were one of a number of tribal groups which inhabited the steppe lands of what is now the republic of Mongolia. Their neighbours, the Tatars, Keraits, Naimans and Merkits were tribes who lived very similar lives and there must have been a certain balance between the groups. Until the beginning of the thirteenth century, the Mongols were scarcely known outside their homelands. All this changed, however, with the career of Temüchin, later known as Genghis (or Chinggis) Khan, probably born around 1170. He is said to have been descended from a family of khans but his father had been poisoned by

'Surrender', from the Scroll of the Mongol Attack *attributed to Tosa Nagataka (Japanese thirteenth century). The Mongol attempt to mount a seaborne invasion of Japan in 1281 met with a humiliating reverse when a storm destroyed the fleet; Japanese artists commemorated this in a series of victory paintings.*

THE MONGOLS BEFORE GENGHIS KHAN

The Mongols were originally just one of a number of related tribes but by 1206 they had all been united under Genghis Khan. Expansion began first against the Xiaxia and the Chin Empire of northern China. Only after they were subdued did Genghis turn west to the Kara Khitay and eventually to Iran and Russia.

members of the rival Tatar tribe and the young Genghis was brought up by his mother in conditions of desperate hardship and poverty. He soon distinguished himself by his ability and his ruthlessness. Slowly, by making alliances and playing off one patron against another, he made himself the leader of the Mongols. Next he launched attacks on the other tribes of the steppes, subduing the Merkits and the Naimans and almost exterminating the Tatars in a fearsome massacre. By 1206 he was master of the steppes and all the other tribes had submitted to his authority.

Compared with Turkish people further west, Mongols seem to have led a very pure nomad life. All the characteristics we have noted in the case of the Turks were here in an exaggerated and intensified form. The Mongols lived off their horses and flocks. Commentators always remarked on the extreme hardiness (and sometimes on the ugliness) of these sturdy ponies. There is a record of a

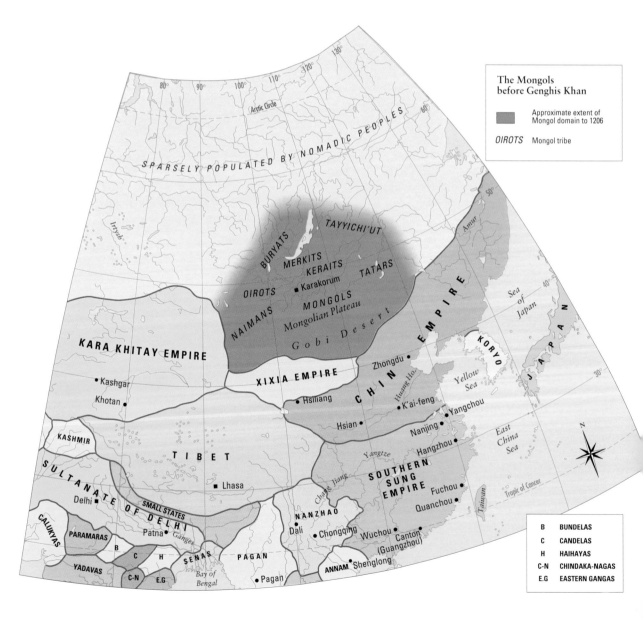

The Mongols
before Genghis Khan

Approximate extent of
Mongol domain to 1206

OIROTS Mongol tribe

B	BUNDELAS
C	CANDELAS
H	HAIHAYAS
C-N	CHINDAKA-NAGAS
E.G	EASTERN GANGAS

A portrait of Genghis Khan from the imperial Chinese portrait gallery in Taiwan. Here Genghis is shown as the first of a long line of Chinese rulers rather than as a Central Asian nomad chief. China was the Mongols' first target after Genghis had achieved power over the steppe tribes in 1206.

Mongol on a single horse covering 600 miles in nine days. Genghis Khan's army once travelled 130 miles in two days, moving without a break. This astonishing mobility was to prove one of their most terrifying features and one of their most important military advantages. They could also move without needing to carry their fodder. In 1241 the emperor Frederick II wrote to his fellow rulers in western Europe to warn them against the Mongol invasions and to try to gather their support. His description of the Mongols and their methods of warfare is surprisingly well informed. Among their strengths he notes that 'when fodder fails them, their horses are said to be satisfied with the bark and leaves of trees and the roots of herbs which the men bring with them: yet they always find them to be very swift and strong in case of necessity'. Other commentators noted that Mongol horses knew how to dig down through the snow to find food whereas horses brought up in more comfortable conditions were unable to cope in the same way.

Like the Turks, the Mongols could survive off a diet of animal products. They drank the milk and ate the flesh of their horses, and we even have accounts

Mongols on their small tough ponies compete in a game of buzbashi, *where different teams struggle for possession of a headless goat's body. Like hunting, this sport is also a training in the skills of horsemanship and warfare.*

Pastoral life on the Central Asian steppes has changed little since the time of Genghis Khan. Here a yurt is pitched beside an animal corral on the vast open plains, warm enough in the summer but bitterly cold during the winter months.

Mongols moving camp,
from a fifteenth-century
Persian miniature. A yurt
still stands with a cooking
cauldron outside at the
bottom left. Elsewhere tents
and bedding are rolled up,
while at the top the tribe
moves off with all its gear
firmly lashed to pack
animals.

of the Mongols drinking the blood of their riding animals in times of great hardship. Their travelling supplies might consist of dried milk curd, to which water was added to make it drinkable, and cured meat. In moments of relaxation they enjoyed the famous *kumiz* or fermented mare's milk. In contrast, the Mongols never practised agriculture and although they certainly ate grain products when available, they had no understanding of farming or sympathy with farmers. Mongol armies needed pasture as twentieth-century armies needed oil and petrol. If the land was occupied by buildings or tillage, then it had to be cleared. They had no interest in preserving orchards or irrigation canals, and needed no urging to convert the land to grass. Equally, Mongol armies could not maintain themselves in the absence of broad pastures. In India, and in the arid lands of southern Iran and Syria, the Mongol advance faltered and halted. In southern Russia and northern Iran, by contrast, extensive grazing meant that their armies could 'refuel' and multiply.

The Mongols also used wagons for transport. Unlike the Islamic Middle East, where wheeled transport was virtually unknown in the Middle Ages, the people of the steppes utilized them for carrying their tents, and necessary household equipment. Wagons were sometimes used on military campaign and wagons are mentioned, for example, in the 1241 battle of Mohi against the Hungarians when they were moved into a circle to provide a sort of improvised fortification. The Mongols were also adept at building rafts to cross rivers: Frederick II in his letter notes, 'They are incomparable archers and carry skins artificially made, in which they cross lakes and the most rapid rivers without danger.'

The bow was their principal weapon. The Mongol version was a composite bow of bone and sinew on a wooden frame. These bows had a very heavy pull, stronger even than the famous English longbows of the later Middle Ages. The effective range could be well over two hundred yards. What is astonishing, however, is that this formidable weapon was used from the back of a swiftly moving horse. Mongols could also fire with terrifying rapidity. When sources talk of the sky becoming dark with their arrows, this was no mere figure of speech. Like an aerial bombardment in modern warfare, it prevented the enemy from manoeuvring or regrouping at will. Of all the nomad peoples of Asia, the Mongols were the most successful in the practice of mounted archery.

Life on the Mongol steppes was very hard and enemies were treated with the most extreme ruthlessness: there was none of the quasi-chivalry which characterized the Bedouin society of the period before Islam. Enemies could be surprised, poisoned (a technique which would have been regarded with the utmost horror by the Bedouin) or have their backs broken. Their women and children could be slaughtered or become the absolute property of the victors. It was a peculiarity of the Mongol scale of values that the shedding of blood was considered especially shameful for the victim. Hence men of high rank would be executed by trampling or suffocation rather than with the sword. This doubtful privilege might even be extended to distinguished outsiders, like the last 'Abbasid

A Mongol going out hunting. Note the quiver with its complement of arrows and the bow on the far side. He wears a turban, which suggests he is a Muslim, a long robe belted at the waist and short leather boots. Note too the care which has been taken to decorate the trappings of the horse and bind its tail. From an anonymous fifteenth-century drawing.

caliph of Baghdad who in 1258 was rolled up in a carpet and trampled to death by horses.

Unlike other nomads, the Mongol soldiers underwent systematic training. This was not done in camps or barracks but on the hunting field. The Mongol leaders mounted great annual hunts, called *nerge*, to provide meat for the winter. A huge ring of hunters would gradually close in on the game, driving it ever closer together. Anyone who allowed an animal to escape would face punishment. As the ring contracted so the press of animals would become more intense. Finally, when the khan gave the order, but not a moment before, the slaughter would begin. The *nerge* inculcated basic skills of teamwork, communication and co-ordination, of encircling the prey and above all, of obedience, which were to be key factors in the success of the conquests.

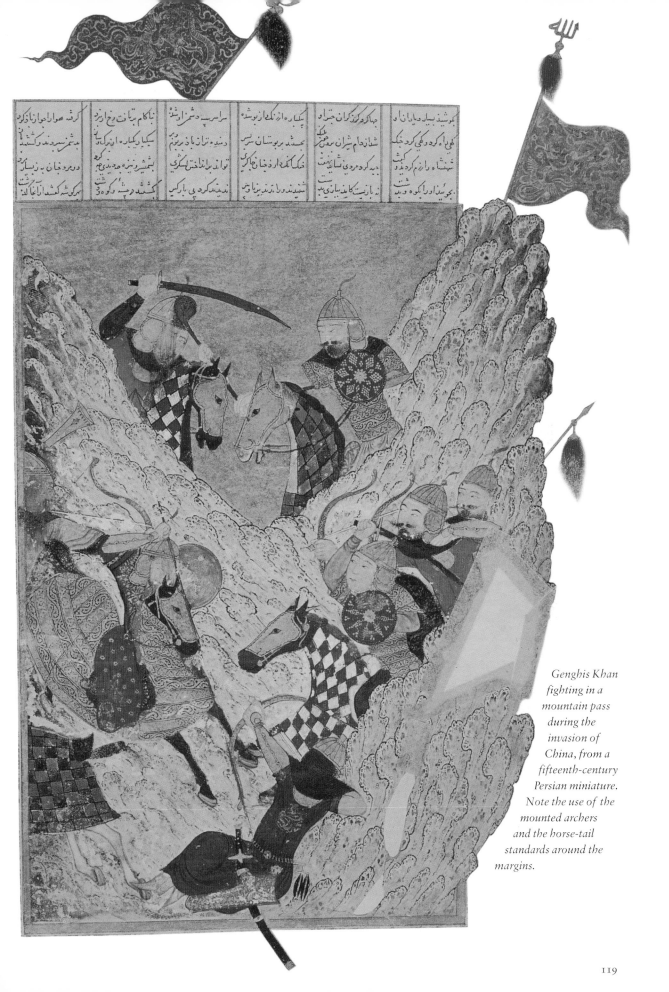

بكوشيد بياد ديان ناه | جباكه كردكردان جنواد | يكباره از بلك ازبوشه | سراسريه دشتراوتش | بناكام بيات رخ ازيزد | كرفه صواراهوازن ازكرد

هرابكه دوكى كردجنگ | شدازدام شيران سوش | بحسنده ريوستان سر | سكبادكبارانلبكان | ميشز سربدبند كسشنه

شنشاه راازم كرده دود | بيدكرده مردى نشانيت | توازراالخذن لبكرى | لشميرونيزه بحينده چم | دومزدخيان يزبيزد

بچوشيد وراكوه دشت | شنيدندورا زندبنارليم | شيانيت كانيذبازيدبيد | كشتده درجت دكوه | هبركى شدكشداذاغالدا

Genghis Khan fighting in a mountain pass during the invasion of China, from a fifteenth-century Persian miniature. Note the use of the mounted archers and the horse-tail standards around the margins.

119

The Persian Juvayni, writing in the lifetime of men who still remembered Genghis Khan, describes his attitude to hunting:

He paid great attention to the chase and used to say that the hunting of wild beasts was a proper occupation for the commanders of armies and that learning about it was essential for them as warriors and soldiers. They should learn how the huntsmen came up with the quarry, how they hunt it, in what manner they array themselves and how they surround it, depending on whether the expedition is large or small. For when the Mongols wish to go hunting, they first send out scouts to see what sorts

Darab (Darius) taken prisoner before Iskandar (Alexander the Great). This miniature of 1410 shows a Turco-Mongol army in action. The weapons used are swords, maces and the typical Mongol composite bow, though Mongol armies are unlikely to have been as beautifully dressed as these. The commander is distinguished by the parasol held over his head.

of game are available and whether it is scarce or abundant. When they are not engaged in warfare, they are very eager for the chase and encourage their armies to take part, not just for the sake of the game but so that they may become accustomed to hunting and familiar with the handling of the bow and the endurance of hardships.

When the Khan sets out on the great hunt (which takes place at the beginning of the winter season) he issues orders that the troops stationed around his headquarters and in the neighbourhood of the camps [the word used for camp, *ordu*, is the origin of the English word horde, used to describe a large group of Mongols] should make preparations for the chase, mounting several men from each ten in accordance with instructions and distributing such equipment in the way of arms and other things as are suitable for the area in which they want to hunt. The right wing, the left wing and the centre of the army are drawn up and entrusted to the great amirs; they then set out with the royal ladies and the concubines as well as provisions of food and drink

For a month or two or three they form a hunting ring and drive the game slowly and gradually before them, taking care lest any escape from the ring. If, unexpectedly, any game should break through, a minute inquiry is made into the cause and the reasons, and the commanders of the thousands, hundreds and tens are clubbed for it and often put to death. And if, for example, a man does not keep to the line but takes a step forward or backward, he is severely punished.

For two or three months by day and by night they drive the game in this manner, like a flock of sheep and send messages to the Khan to inform him of the condition of the quarry, its scarcity or plenty, and where it has come from. Finally when the ring has been contracted to a diameter of two or three parsangs [about nine to twelve miles] they bind ropes together and throw felts over them while the troops come to a halt around the ring standing shoulder to shoulder ... When the ring has been so much contracted that the wild beasts are unable to move, first the Khan rides in with some of his retinue. When he has wearied of the killing, they dismount on some high ground in the centre to watch the princes entering, after them, in due order, the noyans (nobles), commanders and ordinary soldiers. Several days pass in this way.

This account, which is backed by other sources, shows just how much the hunt was a training for war. Obviously it taught the handling of bows but it also taught the skills of communication and co-ordination since it is clear that when the encirclement began, the sides of the ring might be a hundred miles apart and well out of sight of each other. It also taught obedience to the strict rules laid down by the commander: disobedience or failure to carry out one's duty was severely punished. Finally, and perhaps most sinisterly, it ended as a training in

The hunt (nerge) was a major part of Mongol life and military training. In this miniature we see the final stages of a great hunt where the beasts have all been driven together in a confined space and the slaughter has begun. Note the cheetah bottom left and the hawks in the sky, both used in the chase.

mass slaughter. As far as we know none of the other peoples of the steppe hunted in this organized and disciplined way, and indeed the whole process may have been invented by Genghis Khan himself. There could hardly be a clearer explanation as to why the Mongols were so much more effective as conquerors than other tribes with their more disorganized and haphazard campaigns.

By 1206 Genghis had consolidated his hold over the peoples of the Mongolian steppes. Now he set about organizing his supporters into a real military machine. In a great Kuriltay or council held on the Onon river in the heart of Mongolia in the spring he laid down principles of organization which were to become known as the Great Yasa. This was probably never a written law code, as some scholars have maintained, but rather a collection of oral custom laid down by the Great Khan. His first priority seems to have been to break down the tribal structure of the Mongol peoples. As long as the tribe, rather than the khan and the Mongols as a whole, was the main focus of loyalty, the army could never operate as a disciplined fighting force. So the Mongols were divided into units according to the decimal system. Military service was compulsory for all adult males: there were to be no civilians and the Mongol nation genuinely became a nation in arms. The basic unit was a thousand men (*minghan*), ten of which comprised a *tümen* which in turn formed the main divisions of the army. Genghis's children and grandchildren were entrusted with important commands as they came of age and if, and only if, they showed their competence. Otherwise, command of the forces was not given to established tribal leaders but seems to have been based on merit. This meant that talented leaders of modest background, such as Jebe and the great Subedei, whose father was said to have been a blacksmith, could rise by merit to the highest command. Command of units was hereditary from father to son but commanders could be replaced if they were not up to the job. 'If a troop commander is unable to keep his troop ready for battle, he, his wife and his children will all be brought to justice and another leader will be selected from within the troop.'

This military meritocracy may have been an important reason why the Mongols fared so well in battle against armies where military command was regarded as a social distinction to be granted to members of important families rather than a job to be performed professionally and efficiently. Along with this went an equality of lifestyle: the Mongol commanders were expected to share the hardships of their men, to eat the same food and to treat them with firm but equal justice. Outside commentators noted how this ensured they all gave their best and were totally committed to the army and its conquests. For the talented and determined, the highest honours were open, for the incompetent or weak, punishment was swift and often brutal. Blind obedience to the orders of the Great Khan was expected from everyone.

Genghis selected an imperial guard 10,000 strong which was always to be attached to him personally. This élite corps was given special privileges and was clearly distinguished from the rest of the army. 'If an ordinary regimental

commander claims equality with a member of my bodyguard and quarrels with him about this,' Genghis decreed, 'I will punish the regimental commander concerned.' The bodyguard also fulfilled another function. Many of its members were the sons of important military commanders. Under Genghis's watchful eye they could be trained and could develop their loyalty to the Great Khan. They could also, if necessary, be used as hostages for their fathers' good behaviour.

It is doubtful of course that things remained so systematic for long. Like Roman legions, *tümen*s must often have been under strength due to disease or casualties in battle. On the other hand, *tümen*s commanded by successful leaders may well have attracted more recruits, both Mongol and non-Mongol. Far away from the centre, in the forests of northern Russia or the paddy fields of southern China, Mongol commanders must frequently have had to make their own arrangements. None the less, Genghis's administrative arrangements were outstandingly successful. Not only were the Mongols triumphant in every major engagement they fought up to 'Ayn Jalut in 1260, but there was never any problem with tribal rivalries or disobedient and quarrelsome commanders. When division did eventually arise, it was largely due to rivalries between different branches of Genghis's family, not tribal politics or military rebellion. It was in the field of military organization that Genghis's genius really became apparent.

Like the early caliphs of Islam, Genghis realized that in order to keep his following together he had to direct them against outside enemies; and so his career of conquest began. The tribes of the eastern steppes looked to China as the main outside power and it was natural that Genghis should turn his attention to the invasion of China for reasons of plunder and prestige. The first priority was to lead a raid which would result in the capture of flocks and herds as a visible reward for his followers. It was a propitious time for such an expedition.

OPPOSITE: *A sixteenth-century Indian depiction of the Mongol army storming a Chinese city. The achievements of Genghis Khan remained a popular subject for stories and illustrations throughout the Turco-Persian world and the Mogul emperors of India looked to Genghis Khan as their great forebear.*

Mongols torturing their prisoners, from the Great Chronicle *of Matthew Paris (thirteenth century). Though Matthew Paris never left his monastery in St Albans, he was fully aware of the Mongol conquests and their terrible reputation. Here the artist, who of course had never seen a Mongol, imagines the cruelties they practised.*

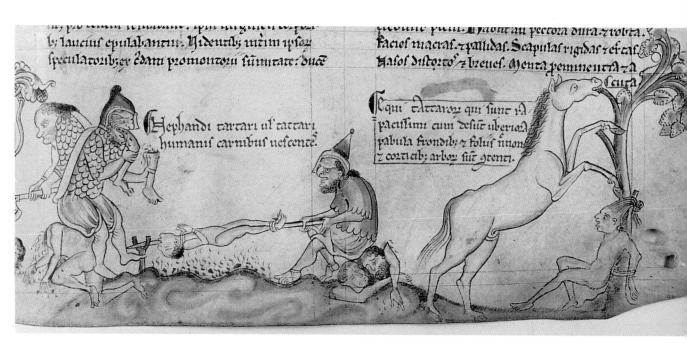

China was divided between two main empires, the Chin of the north and the Sung of the south. The Chin were themselves of nomad origin and their relationship with their Han Chinese subjects was uneasy. To the west of them lived a people the Chinese called the Xixia but whom others knew as the Tanguts. These inhabited the area immediately south of the Gobi Desert with their capital at Ningsia, on the Yellow River. Genghis knew he would have to subdue them to protect his right flank in any invasion of China. A campaign of 1207–8 was no more than a large-scale plundering raid which brought him the booty he needed to keep his followers satisfied. In 1209, however, Genghis embarked on a campaign of conquest of the Tangut Empire, his first operation outside Mongolia. It was also the first time the Mongols had attempted the capture of large fortified towns. Having defeated the main Tangut army, they attempted to take the city of Ningsia by damming the river and flooding it. It was typical of the ambitious and labour-intensive siege works that the Mongols were to undertake elsewhere. However, in the end the dam broke and the Mongol camp itself was flooded. In January 1210 a peace treaty was made by which the Tanguts agreed to pay tribute. It was not a very auspicious beginning to Genghis's career of conquest.

After this, a successful assault on China itself must have seemed vital to preserve his status as a great war leader. He was well aware of the divisions among the Chin and their unpopularity with many of their Chinese subjects. In the spring of 1211 Genghis held a Kuriltay on the banks of the Kerulen river and a campaign was decreed. It was make or break for Genghis. The Chin maintained a formidable army and they were numerically far superior to the Mongols. A setback would certainly have resulted in rebellion by some of his recently subdued enemies in Mongolia itself. Genghis retreated to a mountain-top to pray to heaven while the Mongols fasted for three days and nights. He exhorted them to take revenge for past insults to the Mongolian peoples. The campaign was not easy and at one point Genghis himself was wounded by an arrow but by 1214 the Mongol army was laying siege to the Chin capital Zhongdu, near Beijing. The fall of the city was followed by the first of the great massacres which the Mongols staged to impose their authority. By 1216 Genghis was back in Mongolia, quelling unrest among the remaining Merkit tribesmen, whom he ordered to be massacred to the last man.

The Mongol campaigns in the west can be divided into three phases, each of which showed different aspects of their military talents. First came the initial campaigns of Genghis and his sons in north-eastern Iran from 1219 to 1222 when many of the largest and most prosperous cities of the area were reduced to heaps of smouldering rubble. There followed the extraordinary long-range campaigns of Subedei from 1238 to 1241 in Russia and eastern Europe and finally the campaigns of Hülegü against the castles of the Assassins (1256) and Baghdad (1258), culminating in the Mongol defeat at 'Ayn Jalut in Palestine in 1260.

There is no reason to think that an attack on the West was part of Genghis's

The Great Wall of China. Despite their impressive and sophisticated fortifications, the Chinese armies were unable to resist the highly mobile Mongol forces and Genghis Khan was able to conquer the northern half of the country by 1215.

A war elephant from Rashid al-Din's History *(early fourteenth-century Iran). Elephants could be very effective in battle, especially against foes who had never seen them before, but they were prone to panic and very difficult to feed in the barren lands of Central Asia and the Middle East.*

MONGOL CAMPAIGNS
1206–60

The Mongol campaigns fall into two stages. By the time of Genghis Khan's death in 1227, their armies had conquered northern China and Iran. When after 1236 campaigning resumed, southern China was the target in the East, Russia and eastern Europe in the West.

master plan. But he could not afford to tolerate challenges to his authority and prestige: he still had rivals and sons of dead enemies who would take advantage of any weakness. When in 1218 the governor of the Persian frontier town of Otrar pillaged a caravan travelling the Silk Road under Genghis's protection, it was just such an insult. Worse was to follow when Mongol ambassadors to the governor's superior, the Khwarazm Shah 'Ala al-Din (1200–20), who ruled most of north-eastern Iran, were treated with contempt and one was executed. The next year Genghis visited a terrible vengeance on the Khwarazm Shah and his unfortunate (and blameless) subjects.

Preparations for the campaign began with a vast hunt in the late summer of 1219 in the lands around the river Irtysh, allowing Genghis to train up his forces and giving them the chance to supply themselves with dried meat. In typical Mongol fashion, the attack came in the winter. In February 1220 Otrar was taken. The governor must have expected and certainly received no mercy:

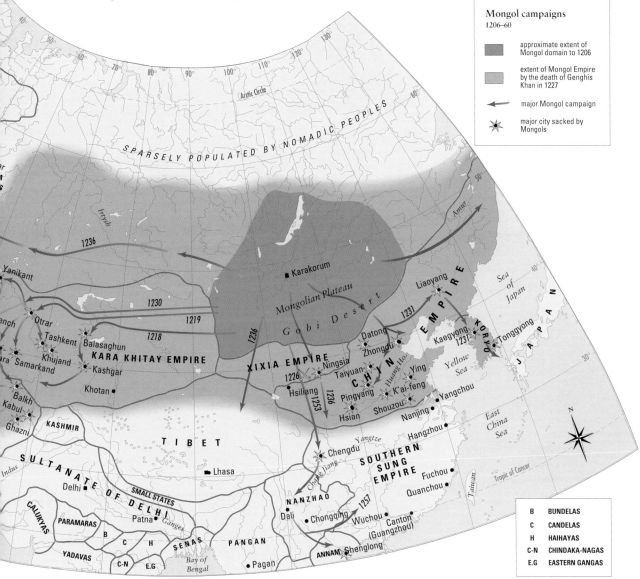

Mongol campaigns
1206–60

approximate extent of Mongol domain to 1206

extent of Mongol Empire by the death of Genghis Khan in 1227

major Mongol campaign

major city sacked by Mongols

B	BUNDELAS
C	CANDELAS
H	HAIHAYAS
C-N	CHINDAKA-NAGAS
E.G	EASTERN GANGAS

according to a Persian historian, he was killed by having molten silver poured in his eyes and ears. Even before Otrar fell, Genghis had moved on the great city of Bukhara, which fell in February or March, and then Samarkand in March. Meanwhile, the Khwarazm Shah fled to an island in the Caspian Sea where he finally met an ignominious end. His more spirited son Jalal al-Din (d. 1231) continued the resistance, fleeing before the Mongol forces to India where he made a dramatic escape, swimming his horse across the Indus to evade his pursuers.

The Mongol armies moved with remorseless determination through Khurasan. Despite considerable damage, Bukhara and Samarkand had been granted terms by the conquerors which allowed urban life to continue. Other cities were not so fortunate. The city of Urgench in Khwarazm (the delta of the Oxus at the south end of the Aral Sea), was taken in fierce hand-to-hand fighting and the inhabitants driven out and enslaved or killed. In February 1221, Merv, the ancient capital of Khurasan, was sacked and left in ruins and two months later Nishapur suffered the same fate. It was only Genghis's renewed preoccupation with events in the east which prevented further advances.

The Mongol armies conquered heavily fortified cities, infinitely richer and more populous than any in their homelands. These cities were ruled by the Khwarazm Shah, the most powerful Muslim ruler of his time, and protected by vast systems of walls. The military historian must ask how they achieved this.

Much of the reason for their success lay in the divisions among their enemies and the complete lack of leadership shown by the Khwarazm Shah. In the whole campaign, there were no major field battles. Rather than summon his armies and lead them against the enemy, the Khwarazm Shah dispersed his troops as garrisons in the cities while he himself fled from one to the other in moods ranging from panic to despair. Most of his troops were Turks and many must have come from nomad backgrounds very similar to the Mongols. Relations between them and the Persian populations of the cities were often uneasy and it was not difficult for the Mongols to find disaffected elements among both the Turkish military and the civilian population who were prepared to treat with them. The failure of leadership was not confined to the Khwarazm Shah alone: Qaracha, deputy commander at Otrar, attempted to flee in the middle of the night with most of his troops but was captured by the Mongols and executed. Baha al-Mulk, appointed governor of Merv, 'made every preparation but when he reached the fortress, he judged it inexpedient to remain there' and fled west, leaving the defence of the city to an inexperienced deputy. But the weaknesses of their opponents can only be part of the explanation.

Sheer weight of numbers may have played an important role. We have several estimates of the total strength of Mongol armies from contemporary or near-contemporary accounts. Mongol sources give fairly believable figures. According to the *Secret History of the Mongols*, the Mongol forces consisted of around 105,000 at the time of the great Kuriltay of 1206, that is before the great conquests got under way. The Persian historian Rashid al-Din, basing himself on

the now lost Altin Debter, says that the army was 129,000 strong at Genghis's death in 1227. Outsiders put the total as much larger and the Persian Juzjani says that 700,000 or 800,000 were involved in the first attack on the Khwarazm Shah. Such enormous figures are very unlikely for simple logistical reasons: even if each Mongol only had two horses, and otherwise lived off the country, that would still mean finding grazing for over a million and a half beasts. A Mongol horde on the move must have been a most impressive sight: a writer such as Juzjani, writing at a safe distance in India and basing his report no doubt on the accounts of fugitives from the defeated armies, may be forgiven for exaggerating.

If we accept the Mongol estimates of slightly over 100,000 as more or less correct, how did this compare with the numbers of their opponents? Persian sources say that the governor of Otrar had 50,000 men under his command and another 10,000 were sent as reinforcements. There was a garrison of at least 20,000 at Bukhara, and after the fall of Samarkand, 30,000 Turkish troops are said to have been put to death by the victorious Mongols. These figures, taken from Juvayni's account written thirty years after the event, and from a Mongol perspective, may be on the high side but the evidence, taken as a whole, suggests that the Mongol armies were not numerically superior to the forces available to the Khwarazm Shah. What is clear, however, is that the enemies of the Mongols remained isolated detachments, which could be picked off one by one. Furthermore, they played a largely static and passive role, waiting behind the protection of the city walls rather than going out to meet the enemy. This may have been a contributing factor in the collapse of morale among the defenders which is so characteristic of the whole campaign.

Most nomad warriors found sieges very difficult to undertake. They lacked the technological know-how and their pastoral lifestyle made staying in one place very difficult. The early Arab conquerors of the Middle East had largely got round this problem by making agreements with townspeople by which they accepted tribute in exchange for not damaging the city. The Mongols, however, showed themselves masters of the hard-fought siege. They probably employed Chinese siege engineers from a very early stage to provide technical expertise, although direct evidence of this is limited.

The most important siege engine was the swing beam catapult or trebuchet, known in Persian as a *manganiq* (from the same root as mangonel). The *manganiq* of the thirteenth century had developed considerably from the hand-powered traction trebuchets of the early Islamic period. The near contemporary illustrations in the Rashid al-Din manuscript show a long beam with the ammunition placed in a sling at the end of it, so that the missile would be accelerated round the end of the beam before being released. At the other end there was a huge box, filled with rock or sand. Apparently a winch or windlass was used to wind the end of the pole down before it was released, perhaps using the sort of catch used on a cross-bow. The construction of these machines was not easy: when the inexperienced defenders of the city of Jand (on the Jaxartes river), who had never had any experience of war, tried to construct one, the stone simply went straight up in the air and landed on the machine itself, totally destroying it. The Mongols usually built siege engines on the sites where they were going to be used (in contrast to the Mameluke sultan Baybars (1260–77). In the 1260s, when he was reducing the great crusader castles, he used to transport his engines from one siege to the next, either whole or in kit form). Naturally, finding the timber was not always easy and at Alamut they used all the fruit trees the inhabitants had planted and tended over the years. Ammunition usually consisted of stones which were ready to hand, but during the bombardment of Nishapur the attackers brought stones with them from several days' journey away. 'These they piled up in heaps like at harvest, and not a tenth part of them were used because the city fell so quickly.' At Urgench, where the alluvial soil of the Oxus delta yielded very little surface stone, they made ammunition out of mulberry wood.

MONGOL SIEGE ENGINE

A city is stormed. Unlike many nomad armies, the Mongols proved adept at siege warfare. From the beginning they employed Chinese and, later, Persian specialists to build machines and thousands of unfortunate prisoners were used as bow and arrow fodder.

The walls of the great cities of Iran were not the vertical stone walls typical of the Mediterranean and northern European cities. They were more like huge clay banks with, perhaps, some fired brick towers and ramparts at the wall-head. We are told that the walls of many cities, Otrar and Samarkand for example, had recently been strengthened. At Merv, where substantial remains of the pre-Mongol fortifications still survive, the brick walls of the Seljuk period, which had interior walkways and chambers in the towers, were drastically modified, probably in response to the Mongol threat. The passages in the walls and the chambers in the towers were all filled up and the thickness of walls and towers greatly increased. These massive works may have been intended to make the walls proof against missiles and to provide firmer bases for the mounting of *manganiqs* by the defenders. Despite the evident effort and expenditure, the fortifications only delayed the fall of the city for a day or two. *Manganiqs* were also used by the defenders; mounted on top of the walls, they could be used to hurl missiles into the attacking army. At Nishapur, the townspeople are said to have had three hundred of them mounted on the wall-heads and towers. They were also used for hurling pots of *naft*. *Naft* or naphtha was essentially crude oil (which comes to the surface naturally in some parts of the Middle East, notably at Baku in Azerbaijan and in central Iraq) and saltpetre. It was used as an incendiary device. In Urgench and Bukhara, towns with a large number of wooden buildings, it was used to fire the residential quarters and spread chaos and confusion. In Samarkand the great old mosque was burned out with it.

Rather than breaching the walls with catapults or undermining them, the Mongols often achieved results by straightforward assault. They often began a siege by approaching the city in small numbers and driving off animals under the eyes of the inhabitants, who naturally gave chase, only to find that they were victims of that traditional nomad trick, the feigned flight. As they pursued what they believed to be a small party of cattle and sheep rustlers, they found themselves ambushed and destroyed. The Mongols then returned in force, sometimes attempting to lure the garrison into making a sortie, more often simply overwhelming the defences by scrambling up the walls. In most cases, it was all over in a day or two: even the mighty fortress of Tirmidh on the Oxus only held out for eleven days.

They also used the *hashar* to great effect. The *hashar* (which signifies a mass

of people but which, in certain contexts, perhaps in deliberate ambiguity, can also mean vermin) was the name given to prisoners of war who had to act as labourers and arrow-fodder for the Mongol armies. When the town of Khojend was taken by the Mongols, for example, the young men were forced into the *hashar* or citadel (the only alternative was instant execution). The citadel lay in the middle of the river so that the captives, with other forced labourers from nearby towns, had to build a causeway in order that the Mongol troops could reach it. 'Fifty thousand levies and 20,000 Mongols were assembled. These were all formed into detachments of tens and hundreds [note again the Mongol attachment to decimal

Mongol warriors, from a manuscript of Rashid al-Din's History *(Persian, fourteenth century). This is probably a training exercise: the archers have dismounted and their opponents are trying to defend themselves with their small round shields.*

divisions]. Over every ten detachments of ten Persians there was set a Mongol officer: on foot they had to carry stones a distance of three parsangs [about twelve miles] and the Mongols on horseback, dropped these into the river.' In this case the *hashar* were comparatively lucky; it may have been hard labour but they were not used as targets of their fellow-countrymen's arrows, as happened elsewhere. In Urgench and Samarkand, for example, the levies were forced to fill up the moat and then begin the demolition of the outer wall right under the noses of the defenders. In Bukhara, after the city had fallen, the local people were driven up to the walls of the citadel until the moat was filled with their dead.

The most potent weapon of the Mongols was terror. To the local people they appeared completely strange and alien; and, unlike other adversaries, they were non-Muslims with no respect for mosques or holy places. Furthermore, with the exception of a small number of artisans, and selected attractive girls and boys, the Mongols did not regard the conquered populations as assets whose talents could be exploited but rather as wasteful occupants of good grazing space and, in addition, potentially dangerous. Other military adventurers would protect a city to enjoy its revenues, if for no more elevated reason. Not so the Mongols, who seem only to have wanted plunder. On a number of occasions when cities were taken, the inhabitants were ordered out into the surrounding plains for six or seven days so that the Mongols could pillage their houses thoroughly and at leisure. If the locals accepted this without resistance or protest, they might be allowed back to the remains of their dwellings.

The survivors, however, were the lucky ones. As the conquest proceeded, the Mongols became even more ferocious. At Bukhara, which was conquered early on, only the Turkish soldiers were systematically slaughtered. At Urgench, where there had been fierce hand-to-hand fighting through the streets, the people were driven out of the city, artisans were separated and taken away, the children and young women were reduced to slavery and 'the men that remained were divided among the (Mongol) army, and to each fighting man fell the execution of twenty-four persons'. After the fall of Balkh (in northern Afghanistan), Genghis Khan commanded that the population, 'small and great, few and many, both men and women should be driven out on the plain and divided up according to the usual custom into hundreds and thousands to be put to the sword; and that not a trace be left of fresh or dry. For a long time wild beasts feasted on their flesh.' After the people of Merv had agreed on terms for surrender,

the Mongols entered the town and drove all the inhabitants, nobles and commoners out on to the plain. For four days and nights the people continued to come out of the town: the

The twelfth- and early thirteenth-century walls of Merv (Turkmenistan). The photograph shows how the twelfth-century walls, with their hollow towers and arrow slits, have been strengthened by a massive outer covering, probably hastily built in the face of the Mongol invasions. It was all to no avail: the city fell without any serious resistance and most of the inhabitants were massacred.

Mongols detained them all, separating the women from the men ... the Mongols ordered that, apart from 400 artisans they specified and selected from among the men and some children, girls and boys, who they bore into captivity, the whole population, including women and children, should be killed, and none, whether man or woman, should be spared. The people of Marv [Merv] were then distributed among the soldiers and levies and, in short, each man was allotted the execution of three or four hundred persons.

The historian Ibn al-Athir was a typical product of the Muslim bourgeoisie of the early thirteenth century. He was immensely learned and well-read and had the ability, not shared by all his colleagues, to demonstrate this learning in simple, straightforward prose. He had visited north-eastern Iran in the years immediately before the Mongol invasions and had been impressed by the size and wealth of the cities and the richness of their libraries. Whether by good luck or good judgement he had returned to his native Mosul (a city never taken by the Mongols) shortly before the storm broke. His appalled reaction to the invasions show the terror the Mongols inspired among people who had never seen them.

Ibn al-Athir tells us:

> I have heard that one of them took a man captive but did not have a
> weapon to kill him with, so he said to his prisoner, 'Lay your head on the
> ground and do not move', and he did so and the [Mongol] went and
> fetched his sword and killed him. Another man told me the following
> story: 'I was going with seventeen others along a road and we met a
> Mongol horseman who ordered us to tie up each others' arms. My
> companions began to do as he said but I said to them, "He is only one
> man, why don't we kill him and escape?" but he replied, "We are afraid."
> I then said, "This man intends to kill you immediately so let's kill him
> and perhaps God will save us." But I swear by God that not one of them
> dared to do this so I took a knife and slew him and we fled and escaped.'
> There were many such events.

Whether the anecdote is true or not, it shows how the sinister reputation of
the Mongols spread. It also highlights a phenomenon known from other war
situations, the passivity and hopelessness which can overcome people when faced
with an enemy they believe to be stronger, leading to a meek acceptance of their
fate. These attitudes provide some insight into the secrets of Mongol success.

The Mongols certainly gloried in and publicized their reputation for terror.
When Genghis Khan took Bukhara, he gathered the survivors in the great
mosque. The scene was one of complete desecration. The chests in which the
great old Qurans were kept had been tipped out so that the leaves were lying
around in the dust while the boxes themselves were used as troughs for the
Mongols' animals. He addressed his cowed audience:

> 'O people, know that you have committed great sins and that the great
> ones among you have committed these sins! If you ask me what proof I
> have for these words, I say it is because I am the punishment of God. If
> you had not committed great sins, God would not have sent a punishment
> like me upon you!' One of his audience told his friend who wanted to
> object, 'Be silent! It is the wind of God's omnipotence that blows and we
> have no power to speak.'

Revisionist historians have questioned the extent of Mongol ferocity and
destructiveness, suggesting that such accounts are largely rhetoric and hyperbole.
However, the weight of contemporary evidence is very strong and it is backed up
by the archaeology. Of the great cities sacked by the Mongols, only Bukhara and
Urgench were rebuilt on the same site: Balkh, Otrar and Nishapur were ruined for
ever and at Merv a new town was founded two centuries later well away from the
remains of the old. Samarkand was rebuilt outside the old walls while the ancient
city remained as it is today, a desolate waste of mud-brick ruins.

Genghis Khan giving his famous 'Punishment of God' speech in the mosque in Bukhara in which he claimed that he was sent by God to punish the sins of the people. Though Genghis was not a Muslim, he is seen here adopting the position of a Muslim preacher on the minbar *or pulpit.*

CHAPTER FIVE

THE MONGOLS IN EUROPE

THE MONGOL ARMY at the battle of Liegnitz (1241). Here we see a Western impression of the Mongols with their pointed caps engaged with the more heavily armoured Christian knights with their great iron helmets. In the end, it was the lighter-armed Mongols who carried the day.

THE MONGOLS IN EUROPE

Saints carved on the exterior of the cathedral at Vladimir. Vladimir was the capital of the most powerful of the eastern Russian principalities at the time of the Mongol invasion and its fall in the campaign of 1237–8 showed the terrifying power of the Mongol armies.

THE MONGOL CAMPAIGNS in Europe have become the archetype, the most commonly quoted example of nomad strategy and warfare. This is partly for the obvious reasons that European scholars were naturally more interested in events nearer home than in the distant plains of Central Asia. Even people in England and France, who had never seen a Mongol, had heard of them; and the image of wild barbarians in the works of chroniclers like Matthew Paris of St Albans ensured that their reputation was kept alive through the centuries. Furthermore, many decision-makers in western Europe were prepared to consider a Faustian bargain with the Mongols. Following the old adage that 'the enemy of my enemy is my friend', they saw the pagan Mongols as possible allies against the Muslims of the Middle East, who were slowly but inexorably destroying the crusader states in the eastern Mediterranean. Some even went further. There was the tantalizing possibility that the Mongols might be converted to Christianity

The image of Prester John, from a medieval map of Africa. Many people in the West believed in a great Christian power in the Far East who would ally with them against Islam. Some kings, like St Louis of France (1228–70), hoped that the Mongols could be converted to Christianity and become allies of the crusaders.

and form a sort of grand coalition to squeeze the Muslim world from east and west. Imaginations ran riot: it was said that the Mongols were connected in some way with Prester John, the mythical Christian monarch from the East (or from Africa, depending on the circumstances) who would come with vast forces to save the Christian cause. Attitudes were very ambivalent: were these invaders simply ruthless and destructive barbarians, or harbingers of salvation for the crusaders and other eastern Christians?

If the optimistic westerners had seen the great army assembled by the Mongol prince Batu (d. 1256), Genghis Khan's grandson, and the general Subedei, veteran leader of the conquests of Iran, assembled on the steppes around the lower Volga river in the autumn of 1237, they would soon have been disabused. There were no signs of crosses or Christian worship here, just a vast army of perhaps 120,000 nomads in search of plunder and rapine.

It is the campaign against Russia and eastern Europe, above all, which established the reputation of the Mongols for mobile warfare. It would be interesting to know more about the logistics of this expedition and the decision-making processes among the Mongol commanders. How much local assistance did they have in finding their way from one city to another? Unfortunately, there are no Mongol sources for this campaign and the Russian annals are short and to the point. Clearly they are more interested in the sufferings of the conquered than in the military skills of the conquerors and whereas we know the route of the Mongol armies and the names of the places they took and the battles they won, we have little more detailed information. Seen as arrows on the map, the movements of the Mongol armies are indeed impressive as they cut swathes through enemy territory, cutting off points of resistance and driving wedges between elements of the enemy forces. This picture of speed and movement

THE MONGOL CAMPAIGNS
IN RUSSIA 1223–40

*The Mongol invasions of
Russia began on the
southern steppes where they
conquered the Turkic tribes,
incorporating many of them
into their armies. In the
winter of 1237–8 they
turned north to eastern
Russia, and in 1239–40 they
devastated western Russia.
The way to Europe lay open.*

appealed enormously to those military thinkers who sought alternatives to the static trench warfare of the First World War. In 1927 Basil Liddell Hart published his book *The Great Captains*, in which he argued that modern tank warfare should follow the Mongol example of swift movements and strikes deep inside enemy territory with encircling movements to dispose of the remaining opposition. This picture is to some extent valid and, as we shall see, Subedei had a clear genius for co-ordinating such long-range warfare. However, the Russian campaign involved elements which Liddell Hart and his colleagues would have been much less keen to claim as their own, notably the systematic use of terror and the exploitation of conquered peoples as slave labour and 'sword fodder' for the army. In this sense, the real heirs of the Mongols were the German armies which invaded Russia in 1941. Without the use of terror, it is unlikely that even Subedei's military genius would have been able to make the conquests he did.

The campaign which led to the attack on Russia and eastern Europe had actually begun the year before, in the summer of 1236. The Mongols always made other nomad tribes their first objective; these were to be defeated and either incorporated into the Mongol armies or exterminated. To the south and east of the settled areas of Russia, two such peoples were to bear the brunt of Mongol attack, the Cumans and the Bulgars of the Middle Volga. The Cumans were Turkic-speaking nomads who roamed the unsettled steppes between the southernmost Russian cities of Pereiaslavl and Kiev and the Black Sea. The Bulgars were, again, a Turkic people who lived in the Middle Volga area to the north of the Caspian Sea. (They were related to those Bulgars who settled the area of modern Bulgaria, but the latter became absorbed in the Slav Orthodox Christian population of the region.)

As Batu and Subedei approached with the Mongol forces, the khan of the Bulgars led his men north along the Volga. Hoping to put water between himself and his horse-borne enemies, he took refuge on an island in the middle of the river (just as the Khwarazm Shah had fled to the island in the Caspian Sea where he died in 1220). He underestimated the thoroughness of his enemy. In one of the manoeuvres that made them so formidable, the Mongols advanced along both sides of the Volga and towed 200 barges each with 100 men up the river itself to prevent him from escaping downstream. The Mongols were certainly brilliant warriors in the traditional steppe lands they knew best, but they also had an extraordinary talent for improvisation and tackling unexpected problems. In the event, the amphibious troops were not required. The horsemen on the banks reached the island and rode across the water by way of a sand-bank. The khan was taken and, too proud to beg for his life, was soon executed.

Other preparations were made for the ensuing operations. The Mongols recruited and trained large numbers of men from the Turkic nomad tribes of the southern Russian and Ukrainian steppes. Whether willingly or as conscripts, they came to join the army. Thus the Mongol army actually increased in size as it moved further from its homelands. Although it no longer consisted solely of

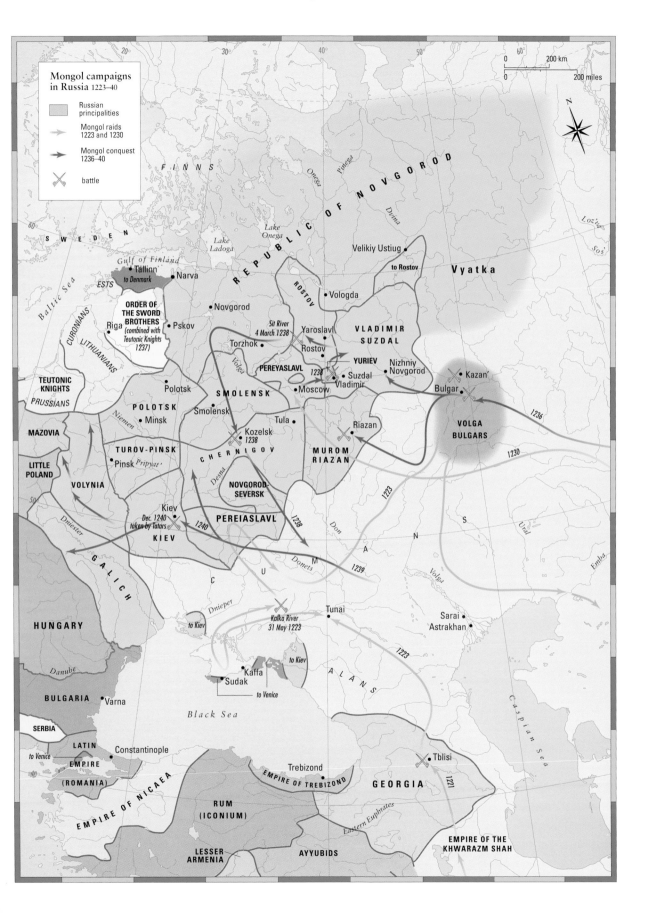

Mongol campaigns
in Russia 1223–40

Russian
principalities

Mongol raids
1223 and 1230

Mongol conquest
1236–40

battle

FINNS

SWEDEN

Baltic Sea

Gulf of Finland
Tallinn
to Denmark
ESTS
Narva

ORDER OF
THE SWORD
BROTHERS
(combined with
Teutonic Knights
1237)

Riga

CURONIANS

LITHUANIANS

TEUTONIC
KNIGHTS

PRUSSIANS

MAZOVIA

LITTLE
POLAND

VOLYNIA

GALICH

HUNGARY

BULGARIA
Varna

SERBIA

LATIN
to Venice
EMPIRE
(ROMANIA)

Constantinople

EMPIRE OF NICAEA

RUM
(ICONIUM)

LESSER
ARMENIA

AYYUBIDS

Lake
Ladoga

Lake
Onega

REPUBLIC OF NOVGOROD

Onega

Pinega

Dvina

Loz

Soš

Velikiy Ustiug

to Rostov

Vyatka

Novgorod

Pskov

Polotsk

POLOTSK
Minsk

Niemen

TUROV-PINSK
Pinsk
Pripyat

Desna

CHERNIGOV

NOVGOROD-
SEVERSK

Kiev
Dec. 1240
taken by Tatars
KIEV

PEREIASLAVL

to Kiev

Dnieper

Kaffa
Sudak
to Venice

Black Sea

Danube

Trebizond

EMPIRE OF TREBIZOND

Vologda

ROSTOV

Sit River
4 March 1238
Torzhok

Smolensk

SMOLENSK

Smolensk

Tula

Kozelsk
1238

Yaroslavl

Rostov

PEREYASLAVL
1238

Moscow

VLADIMIR
SUZDAL

YURIEV

Suzdal
Vladimir

Nizhniy
Novgorod

Kazan'

Bulgar

VOLGA
BULGARS

1236

1230

1223

Riazan

MUROM
RIAZAN

Don

Donets

1238

1239

1240

Kalka River
31 May 1223

Tunai

ALANS

Sarai
Astrakhan

Volga

Ural

Emba

Caspian Sea

Tblisi

GEORGIA

1221

Eastern Euphrates

EMPIRE OF THE
KHWARAZM SHAH

200 km
200 miles

N

pure-bred Mongols, the leadership remained firmly in Mongol hands. Genghis Khan himself had begun this pattern when he incorporated the remnants of the defeated Keraits, Naimans and Tatars into his forces: as in many other ways, his successors were merely following in the great man's footsteps.

The campaign against Russia proper began in the autumn of 1237, when the Mongol horses were fat from the summer grazing. Other invaders of Russia would endeavour to avoid winter campaigns. The intense cold certainly helped to destroy the armies of both Napoleon and Hitler. However, the Mongols deliberately chose to campaign in winter. Accustomed as they were to the freezing steppe lands of Mongolia, they were undeterred by the Russian cold. Their commanders knew that the frozen rivers would give them much greater mobility than the narrow paths and muddy tracks of summer. These would serve as highways through the forest, providing easier access to most of the cities which were their objectives, lying as they did on the river banks.

The lower Volga in spring when the ice has melted and the river is in flood, threatening nearby settlements. The Mongols were keenly aware of the dangers that flooded rivers posed to their communications: in the spring of 1238 the attack on Novgorod was aborted when the thaw began.

As always, intelligence played a vital part in the success of the campaigns. Not only did the Mongols have a clear idea of the geography of Russia, they also understood much about the policies and rivalries of the various princes. Early thirteenth-century Russia was divided into numerous principalities. Although the principality of Kiev was nominally the greatest, its real power had declined considerably since the glorious days of the eleventh and early twelfth centuries: new princedoms like Vladimir Suzdal in the north-east and Volynia in the west were now stronger. There was no longer a central power to co-ordinate resistance. Each principality was effectively on its own against invaders. Many of them, such as Riazan, the first victim of the Mongol attacks, suffered from fierce rivalries within the ruling house. From the time of Genghis Khan onwards, the Mongols were adept at discovering and exploiting the differences among their enemies.

The army which set out that autumn for the northern forests may have numbered as many as 120,000 men, probably as many as Genghis Khan had assembled for the great Kuriltay of 1206 which marked the effective beginning of the Mongol Empire. It was certainly vastly greater than any that the Russian

The Mongols invaded Russia during the winter. The bitter cold held no terrors for them and they could use the frozen rivers as highways through the forests. For the Russians, the icy weather added further hardship and many who managed to escape the Mongol armies must have perished of cold.

principalities could put into the field. The grand strategy was clear, to drive a wedge between the north-eastern principalities and Kiev in the west. The first city to bar their way was Riazan, capital of a weak and divided principality on the fringes of the steppes. It was only a few days before Christmas and the snow must have been thick on the ground. The inhabitants were defiant and shut themselves in their city, hoping no doubt that the Mongols would prove as ineffectual at siege warfare as most nomad peoples. They were mistaken. In nine days the Mongols had surrounded the city with a wooden stockade, to prevent escape and provide shelter for their own men. Then the bombardment began. Five days later the city fell by assault. The buildings were put to the flames, and the prince and his court killed along with most of his subjects: when they were captured they were flayed or impaled. Occasionally the Mongols showed respect for religious buildings and priests and monks. In Riazan no such grace was given. The churches were burned and the clergy killed. According to the horrified accounts in the Russian chronicles, the Mongols also systematically raped nuns and all the young women they could lay their hands on. For the few survivors who did manage to escape, the winter forests must have been a grim and cruel refuge. Undoubtedly the invaders intended the news of this most brutal sack to be spread far and wide to discourage further resistance.

The walls of the old Kremlin at Novgorod (east of St Petersburg). The oldest and greatest of the Russian trading cities was saved, not by the strength of its fortifications, but by the thaw of the spring of 1238 which forced the Mongol armies to retreat.

The Grand Duke of Vladimir Suzdal, the most powerful prince in north-east Russia, now realized that his domains were directly threatened. He sent his son Vladimir to reinforce the garrison at the most southerly of his possessions, the small city of Moscow. Moscow soon fell, leaving Vladimir among the prisoners. The Grand Duke led his army out to confront them but in a manoeuvre which demonstrated once again their terrifying capacity for swift action, the Mongol army bypassed him and rode the 100 miles to the capital at Vladimir without halting. In the Grand Duke's absence, the city was held by his wife and two of his other sons. They were ordered to surrender and forced to watch as their brother, the captured Vladimir, was killed beneath the city walls. The assault began in earnest on Saturday 7 February. The Mongols showered rocks on the city and brought up their battering rams. By Sunday

morning they had already entered the city. The young princes died in the fighting while the duchess and many of her subjects took refuge in the cathedral. If they believed that the holy icons would save them, or that the Mongols would respect the sanctity of a religious building, they soon realized their mistake. The invaders put the church to the flames and all those inside perished.

After the fall of Vladimir, Subedei divided his forces. He himself pursued the Grand Duke, who was still at large with his army, while Batu set off for the great northern trading city of Novgorod. By 4 March Subedei had achieved his objective: the Grand Duke's army was surrounded like the prey at the *nerge*. There were very few survivors. Batu was less successful. As he approached Novgorod, the thaw began. As always, the Mongols were terrified of being caught in unfamiliar territory. The commanders took no risks and retreated through the ravaged lands to the southern steppes where they could recuperate through the summer.

In 1239 the army was once more on the move, first against the remaining nomads of the southern steppes and then against the cities of south-western Russia, the modern Ukraine: Pereiaslavl fell in March and Chernigov in October. The way lay open for an attack on the most ancient and magnificent of Russian cities. They arrived outside Kiev in the autumn. Refugees from far and wide had taken shelter inside the city: 'The Tatar forces besieged the city and it was impossible for anyone to enter or leave,' wrote a Russian chronicler some years after the event. 'Squeaking of wagons, bellowing of camels, sounds of trumpets and organs, neighing of horses and crying and sobs of an innumerable multitude made it impossible for people in the city to hear each other talk. The entire country was overflowing with Tatars.' Resistance, led by the commander Dmitri, was fierce but princes of Kiev had succeeded one another in quick succession in the years before the invasion and none of the contenders for the title remained in the city in its hour of need.

As usual the Mongols sent a messenger demanding surrender: as usual the defenders rejected these overtures. The Mongols began the attack on a section of the defences by the Polish gate where the walls were made of wood. The Mongol

assault began with volleys of arrows: 'Arrows obscured the light and because of this it was impossible to see the sky but there was darkness from the number of Tatar arrows.' The battering rams got to work on the walls and soon the Mongols began to pour into the city. With strength born of desperation the inhabitants set up another line of makeshift defences around the Church of the Virgin but this too soon fell and hundreds of the hapless citizens were crushed or suffocated in its ruins. It was St Nicholas Day, 6 December. When resistance was over the wounded commander, Dmitri, was brought before Batu and, most unusually, was pardoned on account of his bravery and allowed to go free. It seems to have been a classic Mongol victory: their vast numbers, the effect of their archery, their determination with siege engines and their abilities as street-fighters all contributed. Again, too, they benefited from the lack of a co-ordinated and determined resistance. Had they been confronted by a single, united, well-led Russian army, their military record might have been much less impressive.

In the aftermath of the fall of Kiev, other cities in western Ukraine were soon destroyed. Batu collected his forces at Przemysl, now in south-eastern Poland. Here Subedei planned the last and most daring of his military campaigns. Subedei's forces may have amounted to 100,000 men but even with this large number his strategy was extremely bold. He proposed sending the main part of the army across the Carpathian Mountains into Hungary. There were good reasons for choosing Hungary. Many Cumans opposed to the Mongols had taken refuge there and the young king Bela IV might prove a formidable opponent. The Mongols could not press further west while he remained at large. They must have known too that Hungary, unlike lands further to the north and west, offered abundant grazing. It was after all on these steppes that Attila had made his base eight hundred years previously, attracted by the same grasslands. Hungary could be a base for further raids and a place for the Mongols and their horses to rest and recuperate. Meanwhile, a small force, said to have been two *tümens*, or about 20,000 men, was despatched to secure the northern flank of the army, through what is now southern Poland.

It is impossible not to be impressed by the scope of Subedei's strategic vision in his conduct of long-range co-ordinated movements. The whole plan depended on maintaining contact and synchronicity between armies operating up to 600 miles apart in largely hostile country. His intelligence must have been excellent. Not only was he fully informed of the geography and the possible routes, but he seems to have had a clear idea of the tensions at the

Kiev (Ukraine) in a nineteenth-century photograph. The ancient political and ecclesiastical capital of Russia was sacked on St Nicholas' Day, 6 December 1239, after fierce resistance. Unusually, the Mongol commander Batu spared the Russian commander Dmitri as a tribute to his bravery. The city never regained its leading position in Russia.

court of Bela between the young king, his rebellious barons and the Cuman allies he had welcomed.

Bela ordered that the Carpathian passes be fortified and in the spring of 1241 he assembled his army at Buda, the fortified city overlooking the Danube which was to become half of Budapest. On 14 March he was told that the Mongols had forced the Carpathian passes and were pressing on through the snow at speeds of up to 50 miles a day. But the position was even worse than the young king realized. For while Batu and the main army were advancing from the west, Subedei had led a long-range group through the plains of Romania and up the Danube valley to attack Hungary from the south. By the end of March, the Mongol armies had reunited and were drawn up near Pest. The fearful king despatched his wife to the safety of Austria, while the barons demanded privileges and the expulsion of the Cumans before they would fight. All seemed set for a major confrontation at Budapest when the Mongols suddenly withdrew.

The feigned retreat was a classic nomad manoeuvre and it seems clear that Subedei and Batu planned to lure Bela away from his base at Buda into more favourable terrain. They retreated to the north-east, to make sure that they could escape into the Russian steppes if things went wrong. On 10 April the Mongols stopped near Tokay on the southern fringes of the mountains. Batu selected a site, a heath with rivers and marshes on three sides and the mountains and forests behind. Here they made a camp, surrounding the tents with hundreds of wagons held together with chains and ropes (very reminiscent of Attila's fortified camp at the Catalaunian Plains). It was a perfectly laid trap. That night Subedei led 30,000 men round behind the Hungarian army. If intelligence was one of the Mongols' great strengths, it was one of the Hungarians' greatest weaknesses; Bela was completely unaware that he was surrounded.

The forested slopes of the Carpathian Mountains in northern Hungary. The Mongols constantly surprised their enemies by their ability to move swiftly through all sorts of terrain. Many in Hungary believed that the mountains would protect them from the Mongol armies in the Ukraine but they were soon proved wrong.

MONGOL CAMPAIGNS IN EUROPE 1240–45

Two Mongol armies set out to invade Europe: one went west through the plains of Poland, defeating Henry of Silesia at Liegnitz in 1241; the other headed south-west through the Carpathians to attack Hungary while Subedei led a pincer movement along the Danube to take the Hungarians in the rear. Speed and co-ordination were the characteristics of Mongol military strategy.

Mongols campaigns
in Europe 1240–45

→ main attack

→ flank attack

→ reconnaissance
and minor raids

⚔ battle site

to Denmark

NORWAY

Stockholm

SWEDEN

ESTONIANS

TEUTONIC
KNIGHTS

REPUBLIC OF
NOVGOROD

CURONIANS

DENMARK

LITHUANIANS

POLOTSK

Dnieper

TEUTONIC
KNIGHTS

POMERELIA

PRUSSIANS

TUROV-PINSK

Baltic Sea

Vistula

GREAT
POLAND

MAZOVIA

LITTLE
POLAND

VOLYNIA

Vladimir

Chernigov

KIEV

Kiev

1239

Liegnitz
Breslau
Silesia

Cracow

Przemysl

Mongol army
concentrates here
January 1241

Galich

1240

CUMANS

Kingdom of

Germany

1241

Prague

Kingdom
of Bohemia

Carpathian

1241

GALICH

1241

Dniester

HOLY

1241

Mohi

1241

1241

1243

Danube

Vienna

Buda

ROMAN

M t s

EMPIRE

HUNGARY

Zagreb

1241

1242/43

Belgrade

Black
Sea

Venice

Dinaric Alps

Bosnia

Varna

Kingdom
of Italy

Ravenna

SERBIA

Nis

BULGARIA

Florence

Adriatic Sea

Ragusa

1242

Constantinople

PAPAL STATES

Rome

DESPOTE
OF
EPIRUS

KINGDOM
OF SALONIKA

Salonika

LATIN
EMPIRE
(ROMANIA)

Bari

EMPIRE
OF
NICAEA

Naples

Taranto

Janina

Aegean
Sea

RUM
(ICONIUM)

Tyrrhenian
Sea

N

DUCHY
OF ATHENS

Athens

KINGDOM OF SICILY

Palermo

Messina

PRINCIPALITY
OF ACHAIA

VENETIAN
REPUBLIC

Catania

Mediterranean Sea

0   200 km

0   200 miles

Next day Batu's men began to advance. His soldiers were certainly outnumbered by the Hungarian army and he moved cautiously forward. In this slow-moving battle, the Mongols used trebuchet catapults not against cities or fortifications, but as field artillery. Eight of them were employed and gradually advanced with the troops in a kind of rolling barrage. In addition, they seem to have used incendiary ammunition, creating 'thunderous noise and flashes of fire' probably made by jars or cauldrons full of heated oil.

As Batu's men slowly advanced the Hungarians must have felt fairly confident that they could defeat this smallish force, but then Subedei's men appeared from behind and they were showered with arrows from both sides. However, they did not panic but fortified themselves in a camp. The Mongols then turned their attention to this camp, which was burned out after being bombarded by the artillery. Hungarian morale now cracked. Many, including the king, made a dash for the few gaps in the Mongol lines and rode into the mountains. Some, like the contingent of Knights Templars, stood their ground and fought to the last man. It was one of the Mongols most spectacular victories in battle but it had cost them many casualties. They established themselves in Hungary to recover and gather their resources: they minted coins and encouraged the peasants to return to their fields. The sacrifice of the Hungarian army may well have saved Austria and Italy from their invasion.

At Mohi, too, tensions began to become apparent among the Mongol leaders. Batu was clearly very anxious about the outcome of the battle. His scouts said that the Hungarian army was twice the size of his own. According to one source he went up to a hill-top and, 'for one day and night he spoke to no one but prayed and lamented and he ordered the Muslims (in his army) to assemble

THE BATTLE OF MOHI 1241

The Mongol victory at Mohi showed once again their capacity for manoeuvre and encirclement. But it also showed their skill at intelligence gathering. They were always better informed than their enemies, even about dissension and quarrels within their opponents' ranks.

The battle of Mohi
1241

Phase 1

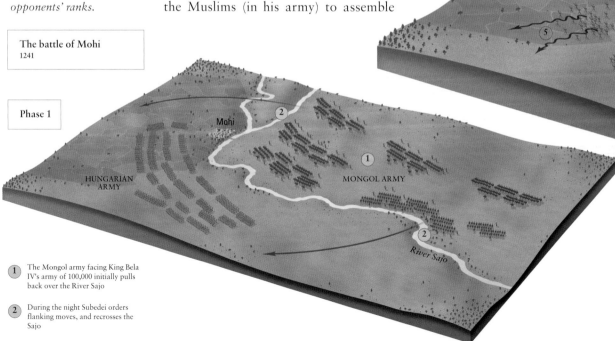

1 The Mongol army facing King Bela IV's army of 100,000 initially pulls back over the River Sajo

2 During the night Subedei orders flanking moves, and recrosses the Sajo

and pray as well'. In the course of the fighting he seems to have lost his temper with Subedei, blaming him for being too slow to lead his forces into battle and having thus caused him to lose many men. He brought the subject up again at a banquet in Pest, accusing Subedei of holding back. But Subedei excused himself by saying that the river he crossed was deeper than expected and it had taken him longer to construct the bridge. Finally Batu relented and offered him a cup of wine saying, 'Everything we have achieved we owe to Subedei.' The stories may be apocryphal but they are still interesting. For virtually the only time in the narratives of the Mongol conquests, their commanders appear as real human beings, stressed and anxious and taking it out on those closest to them when things did not work out as planned.

Meanwhile, the northern army had been cutting a swathe through southern Poland. Here, as in Russia, they found a land divided up among many different princes who proved unable to unite against the invasion. There had not been a king of Poland since 1138, a century before, and there was no individual to lead the nation against the invaders. The intention of the expedition seems to have been to create a diversion and prevent any of the Polish or German princes

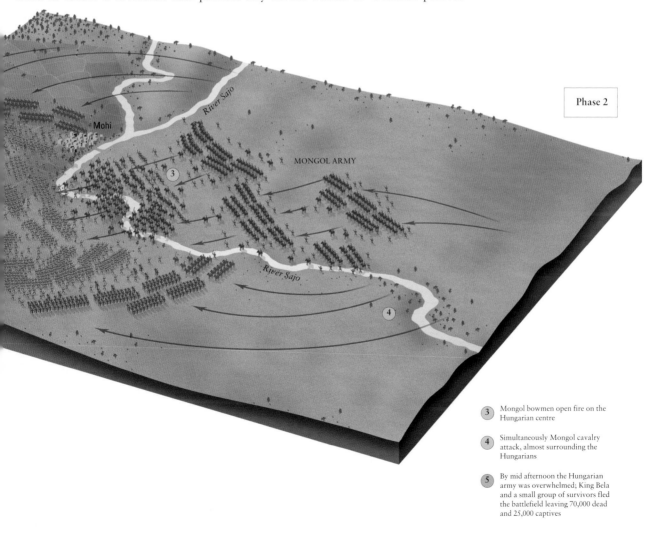

Phase 2

3 Mongol bowmen open fire on the Hungarian centre

4 Simultaneously Mongol cavalry attack, almost surrounding the Hungarians

5 By mid afternoon the Hungarian army was overwhelmed; King Bela and a small group of survivors fled the battlefield leaving 70,000 dead and 25,000 captives

coming to the aid of the Hungarians. The Mongol general, Baidar, approached Cracow early in the spring of 1241. Cracow was the stronghold of Boleslav the Chaste, who was likely to prove the strongest of the Polish princes. When they were outside the walls Boleslav led a sortie and the Mongols turned and fled, as if defeated. Once again, their enemies were taken in by the feigned flight. Only a few miles from Cracow the Mongols lay in ambush and the Poles were virtually wiped out by a hail of enemy arrows. Cracow was abandoned by the panic-stricken populace and on 24 March the Mongols entered and burned the city.

The Mongol commanders Baidar and Kadan pressed westward into Silesia.

The Mongols approach the city of Liegnitz after their victory over the army of Duke Henry of Silesia. They are taunting the inhabitants by displaying the head of the duke on a spear. Rather than pressing further to the West, the victorious Mongol army turned south into Hungary.

Here they were confronted by Duke Henry. They also knew that the king of Bohemia and other princes were coming to join him. Henry gathered his forces at Legnica (Liegnitz). There were probably about 25,000 of them. Some were knights in full array and there was a stiffening of Hospitallers, Templars and a larger contingent of Teutonic knights. On 9 April 1241 Duke Henry rode out of the town to confront the enemy. At first his knights seemed to be making progress against the Mongol horsemen in the centre. Encouraged by this, Henry threw all his cavalry into the fray. As they advanced, the Mongol archers moved up on either side of their column. Henry had made the fatal mistake of allowing the

cavalry to be separated from the infantry and the Mongol archers entered the gap that opened up. Smoke from the fires they lit prevented the infantry and cavalry seeing each other; as the Silesian horsemen were tormented and routed by the Mongol archers, the infantry were ridden down and destroyed by their cavalry. Henry himself attempted to flee but was caught and executed. After the battle, the Mongols collected the ears of the slain in sacks and sent them as a gruesome sign of their triumph to Batu in Hungary.

Whether by accident or design, the battle at Liegnitz was fought just two days before the battle of Mohi where Batu and Subedei defeated the Hungarians. The Mongols had won at Liegnitz, but as at Mohi, there had been a heavy cost. Baidar and Kadan then turned south to join the main Mongol army at Pest.

Here preparations were being made for a winter campaign against Austria. There was also unfinished business with Bela of Hungary. The Mongols were always energetic in pursuit of defeated enemy leaders, as the Khwarazm Shah and

OPPOSITE: A French bronze cast showing a typical Western knight of the mid thirteenth century. He has a sheet-metal helmet but is otherwise wearing chain mail under his surcoat. From the position of his arm, he was clearly carrying a lance, the characteristic weapon of the knight.

A nineteenth-century illustration of a Mongol warrior. His costume and equipment would have been familiar to Genghis Khan and his followers. Note the sword, bow-case and arrows. He is warmly clad but has no body armour.

his son Jalal al-Din had learned. Bela fled to Croatia and down the Adriatic coast, finally taking refuge on the island of Trogir. A Mongol force under Kaidar chased after him, but this was not good Mongol country. There was little or no pasture and the local people were decidedly hostile. In the end the pursuit was abandoned and eventually Bela returned to Hungary where he reigned as king until his death in 1270, the longest surviving participant in this drama.

Preparations for the assault on Austria continued. The Danube was frozen and on Christmas Day 1241 the Mongols crossed it and sacked Gran, a major commercial town and seat of the archbishop, with the customary cruelty. Shortly afterwards their scouts were seen in the outskirts of Vienna.

It was at this point that news reached Batu and Subedei that the Great Khan Ogedei (1227–41) had died in distant Karakorum (the Mongol capital). Rivalries

The Great Khan Ogedei (1227–41). His death in the Mongol capital at Karakorum meant that the Mongol leaders in the west, Batu and Subedei, abandoned their plans for further conquests in Europe and returned east to participate in the choice of his successor.

among the descendants of Genghis Khan had been brewing for some time and it was important to be near at hand when decisions were made. So Batu and Subedei made their way, first to Saray on the Volga, where Batu stayed to organize what was to become the Khanate of the Golden Horde, while Subedei took the rest of the army on to Karakorum. Never again did Mongol forces seriously threaten the West.

How far would the Mongols have advanced if the Great Khan had not died at this point? Of course we can never know. Subedei and Batu, the great partners, were clearly disappointed not to be able to press on, and many in western Europe were extremely worried about this new menace. Leaders and messengers scurried around trying to create some sort of united front against them. Yet there are reasons for thinking that the Mongol armies had almost reached their limits. The landscapes were very different from the steppe lands they had left. Finding pasture would certainly be a major problem. Fortified towns and castles were much more numerous, nor were there any nomad tribes they could incorporate into their own to maintain their numbers. Liegnitz and Mohi had both been victories but neither had been easy and the Mongols had sustained heavy losses. Far from their bases and the environment they loved, the Mongol armies would surely have been destroyed by a slow process of attrition if not defeat in battle.

The end of the European campaign in 1241 was not the end of Mongol expansion in the West. Memories of the conquests of Genghis Khan were still very much alive and at the Kuriltay in 1251 the Great Khan Mongke (1251–9) despatched two of his brothers on major wars of conquest. Kubilai was sent to China to conquer the southern Sung and Hülegü was sent to Iran. Hülegü's expedition was a far cry from the impetuous campaigns of Genghis's time. His army was probably larger than the one Genghis had led to the conquest of Iran. It included contributions from many Mongol princes, including Batu, who still held court on the Volga steppes. There were also Chinese siege engineers and shooters of *naft*. His progress was stately and fairly slow. Pasture on both sides of the route was reserved for the army, boulders and thorns were cleared from the roads, bridges and ferries arranged. It was also something of a social occasion and he stopped off to stay with the princess Orqina, widow of Genghis's son Chaghatay (d. 1242) who now ruled over her husband's followers. There was tiger hunting in the bush along the Oxus river and magnificent feasts in huge tents organized by the Mongol governor of Iran, Arghun Aqa.

OVERLEAF: *Karakorum, Republic of Mongolia. Virtually nothing survives of the capital of the great Khans except the stone tortoise. The walls and pinnacles in the background are part of a later Buddhist monastery. While other capital cities are in fertile countryside or on rivers, Karakorum was built in the middle of vast grazing lands, the Mongols' most important resource.*

This coin of Ogedei shows him as a great warrior in the Mongol tradition. In reality, despite the fact that he was Genghis Khan's son and successor, he seldom went on campaign in person and spent much of his reign developing his new capital at Karakorum. It was left to princes like Batu and generals like Subedei to continue the conquests.

But there was also a military objective. Hülegü's first aim was to take the castles of the Isma'ili Assassins. Since the time of the Crusades and Marco Polo, the legendary Assassins have fascinated outside observers. The Isma'ilis had begun as a radical Shi'ite sect in the tenth century. At the end of the eleventh and the beginning of the twelfth century members of the sect in Syria and Iran had been driven from the cities and taken refuge in the mountains of northern Syria and northern Iran. In Iran they had established a series of castles on rugged peaks in remote areas: Alamut and Maymun-Diz north of Qazvin were the most famous. They defended themselves not by maintaining large armies but by the remoteness of their situation and the use of suicide assassins to dispose of enemy leaders. The story went that the Master of the Assassins would attract young men

The Rock of Alamut, northern Iran. These rocks were the site of the Isma'ilis' fabled castle at Alamut. A generation after the rest of Iran had succumbed to the Mongol yoke, the Isma'ilis still resisted in their remote mountain castles. Not until Hülegü's campaign of 1256 were they finally subdued.

to a remote castle. They would be drugged and when they woke up would find themselves in a garden where they were offered all the joys of paradise as described in the Quran. When, exhausted by their pleasures, they fell asleep, they awoke to find themselves on some bleak and stony mountain side. The Master then suggested to them that if they were to carry out a mission, which would inevitably result in their own death, they would enjoy the pleasures they had tasted so briefly for all eternity. Perhaps sadly, the story as it has come down to us is certainly a fabrication put about by their enemies, but the Isma'ili Assassins did use political murder and they did inspire fear and loathing among their opponents.

The reality was that by the 1250s they were much tamer than they had been a century before, yet they still resisted Mongol rule in Iran: as such they had to be exterminated. Hülegü's campaign reveals the Mongol genius for siegecraft. When he arrived in Iran in the spring of 1256, Hülegü demanded that the Master of the

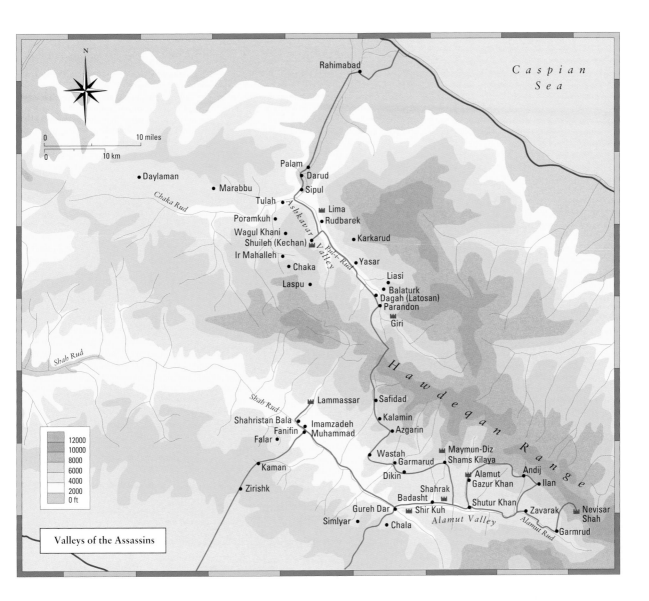

Caspian
Sea

N

0 ——— 10 miles
0 ——— 10 km

Rahimabad

Daylaman

Chaka Rud

Palam
Darud
Sipul
Marabbu
Tulah
Lima
Poramkuh
Rudbarek
Wagul Khani
Shuileh (Kechan)
Karkarud
Ir Mahalleh
Yasar
Chaka
Liasi
Laspu
Balaturk
Dagah (Latosan)
Parandon
Giri

Ashkavar Valley
Pul-i-Rud

Shah Rud

Hawdeqan Range

Shah Rud
Lammassar
Safidad
Shahristan Bala
Kalamin
Fanifin
Imamzadeh
Muhammad
Azgarin
Falar
Wastah
Maymun-Diz
Garmarud
Shams Kilaya
Kaman
Dikin
Alamut
Andij
Gazur Khan
Shahrak
Ilan
Zirishk
Badasht
Shutur Khan
Gureh Dar
Shir Kuh
Zavarak
Nevisar
Shah
Simlyar
Chala
Alamut Valley
Alamut Rud
Garmrud

12000
10000
8000
6000
4000
2000
0 ft

Valleys of the Assassins

Assassins, Rukn al-Din, should surrender his castles. This was met with a polite refusal. A diplomatic game of cat and mouse now ensued as Hülegü made his military preparations. As the Mongol army approached the mountains around Alamut, Rukn al-Din played for time, hoping the winter snows would come in time to save him. He sent hostages and 300 men to serve as *hashar* to demolish the outlying castles. But he still hoped to hang on to Alamut with its magnificent fortifications and the library built up over previous centuries. Hülegü knew he had a struggle on his hands. Supplies were collected from all over north-western Iran, for winter was near and there would be no pasture to be had in these craggy mountains. Flour and animals for transport and slaughter were assembled. On 8 November Hülegü found himself overlooking the castle at Maymun-Diz. The next day he rode around looking for the weak points. He then held a council of war. Many of his commanders were in favour of retreat, given the problems of supply and the deteriorating weather, but a minority, including Kit-Buga, one

VALLEYS OF THE ASSASSINS

The castles of the Isma'ili Assassins lay in the remote mountain valleys of northern Iran. Away from trade routes and major cities they had maintained their independence against all comers for almost two centuries when Hülegü destroyed them in a single season's campaigning in 1256. It was a triumph for Mongol siegecraft.

of his most experienced generals, urged him to press on. He set about making trebuchets, cutting down the great trees which previous generations of Isma'ilis had planted on the surrounding hills. Relays of men were established to transport the beams up to the castle. The defenders in turn set up trebuchets on their ramparts to rain stones 'like falling leaves' on their assailants. As usual, the Mongol attackers responded with clouds of arrows. Chinese siege engineers had constructed a sort of giant crossbow called a *kaman-i gav* (ox's bow) which is said to have been able to shoot arrows up to 2,500 paces. If this is true, then the range must have been at least 2,000 yards, significantly longer than the recorded range of any other pre-gunpowder artillery. However, the historian Juvayni, who was present at the siege, may have got carried away with the excitement of the new technology.

ASSASSIN CASTLE OF ALAMUT

The castle of Alamut, the stronghold of the Master of the Assassins, was a series of enclosures spread out along a steep and barren crag. The Mongols used giant siege engines to intimidate the defenders into surrender. It was in this remote and windswept castle that the Grand Master of the Assassins was said, in popular legend, to have drugged his young followers and showed them all the pleasures of paradise before they were despatched on their suicide missions.

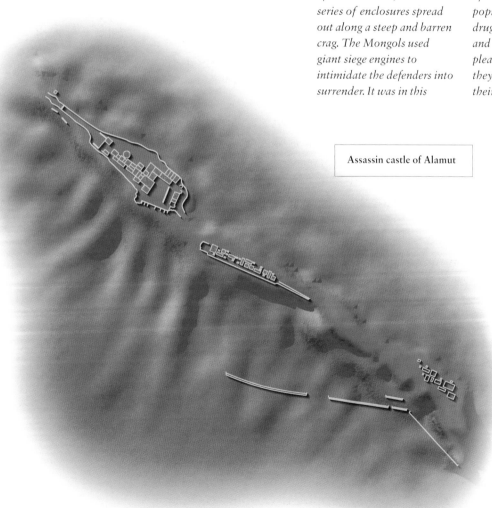

Assassin castle of Alamut

The historian describes the effect of the bombardment:

As for the trebuchets which had been set up it was as though their poles were made of pine trees a hundred years old [that is, they were very strong]. The first stones which were discharged from them broke the defenders' trebuchet and many were crushed under it. Fear of the quarrels from the crossbows overcame them so that they were in a complete panic and tried to make shields out of veils [which is to say that they did their best to defend themselves with very inadequate equipment]. Some who were standing on towers crept in their terror like mice into holes or fled like lizards into the crannies of the rocks. Some were left wounded and some lifeless and all that they struggled feebly like mere women.

Mongol sieges never lasted very long. In the face of this unrelenting bombardment, Rukn al-Din agreed to surrender. It was 19 November.

Even after this, some of the more determined Isma'ilis held out with the courage of desperation for another three nights until, on the fourth day, the Mongol troops entered the castle and began to destroy the buildings, 'brushing away the dust with the broom of annihilation'. Having seen what had happened at Maymun-Diz, the commander of nearby Alamut surrendered after a few days' siege. As Juvayni remarks, in the early twelfth century the Seljuk sultan Muhammad (1105–18) had laid siege to Alamut for eleven years with no result: the Mongols had taken it and all the other castles in just two weeks. There could not be a clearer illustration of the contrast between the determined and efficient Mongol military machine and their more ineffectual predecessors.

The fall of the Assassin castles was just the beginning of Hülegü's plan of conquest. The Mongols never seem to have felt that they had done enough: there were always new lands to raid and subdue until the whole world acknowledged the authority of the Great Khan. The next target was Baghdad, ruled by the 'Abbasid caliph al-Mu'tasim, successor of the Prophet and heir to a line which had ruled since 750. Like the Great Khan, the caliph had pretensions to be ruler of the world, or at least of the whole Muslim world. It was a challenge Hülegü and the Mongols could not ignore.

The reality of the caliph's position was very different. In practice he only ruled the city of Baghdad and the surrounding area. Even the city itself was bitterly divided between Sunni supporters of the caliphate and their Shi'ite opponents, divisions of which the Mongols were, as always, well aware. As the Mongol army approached, the caliph refused once again to acknowledge the Great Khan's supremacy and attempted, belatedly, to repair the defences of the city. The garrison attempted a sortie but were dispersed and many were drowned when the Mongols cut the irrigation ditches. Many in the Shi'ite quarters welcomed the invaders. The bombardment of the fortified city commenced on 30 January 1258. As usual, it was all over quite soon; the walls had fallen by

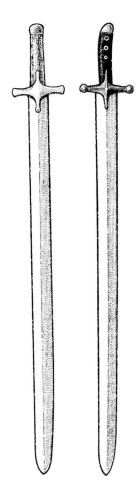

'ABBASID SWORDS

Two swords now in the Topkapı Palace, Istanbul, are said to have belonged to the last 'Abbasid caliph of Baghdad, al-Mu'tasim. When Baghdad fell, he was taken prisoner by the Mongols, rolled up in a carpet and trampled to death to avoid shedding his blood. The swords were probably taken by surviving members of the 'Abbasid family to Cairo and then to Istanbul after 1517 when the Ottoman sultans assumed the title of caliph.

The Mongol conquest of
Baghdad in 1258, from a
Persian manuscript. Note
the trebuchet in the
foreground: by this time the
Mongols had become
masters of the technology of
siege warfare. The Mongol
conquest was followed by
the slaughter of thousands
of the inhabitants and the
destruction of many ancient
libraries in the city.

6 February. The misguided citizens streamed out, believing that they had been granted their lives. They were soon undeceived as the Mongols began the systematic slaughter. The caliph himself was taken to Hülegü's camp, taunted and mocked and eventually rolled in a carpet and trampled to death.

The fall of Baghdad caused deep shock in the Muslim Middle East but it did not put an end to rivalries between the Ayyubid rulers of Syria and the Mameluke soldiers who were now the effective power in Egypt, not to speak of the last crusader outposts whose inhabitants were divided between those who saw the Mongols as deliverers and those who regarded them as a menace. Hülegü pressed on. Early in 1260 Aleppo was taken, the men were slaughtered and the women and children made slaves. The country was gripped by panic and local rulers had no effective response.

Once again the Mongol advance was halted by events far away. News arrived that the Great Khan Mongke was dead. Hülegü, who may have hoped to succeed him, retreated with most of his troops to Iran, leaving his Christian general Kit-Buga in Damascus with an army of perhaps 25,000, many of whom were not Mongols but conscripts from Georgia and Armenia. Meanwhile the military strong man of Egypt, the Mameluke Kutuz, arrived with perhaps 100,000 troops to prevent further Mongol advances. On 3 September 1260 the two armies met at 'Ayn Jalut (Goliath's Spring) just west of the Sea of Galilee. Although their army was seriously outnumbered, the Mongols decided to take the initiative: the main force engaged the Mamelukes on a broad front while a detachment was sent to make a sweep around the right wing and so take the enemy from the rear. Kutuz was a competent commander and kept his head, eventually using his superiority in numbers to surround the Mongol army. Kit-Buga seems to have died fighting and the survivors fled east across the Jordan.

At one level the defeat at 'Ayn Jalut was only a setback. The Mongol army was small, consisting largely of foreigners. The great hordes in Iran and Russia were still intact and Hülegü could strike again. However, events were to

MONGOL CAMPAIGNS IN ASIA c. 1300

After about 1260 the Mongol Empire, though theoretically all one state, began to divide into different areas. The Great Khan Kubilai based himself in China and became effectively a Chinese emperor, while his brother Hülegü established an independent state in Iran. Other members of the family founded the Chaghatai Khanate in Central Asia and the Khanate of the Golden Horde in southern Russia.

prove that it was the high-water mark of the Mongol advance. The myth of their invincibility was shattered and it had been proved that a large, well-led conventional army could defeat them. But there were other factors too: the hot deserts of Syria and Egypt did not offer the grazing the Mongols needed to sustain their war effort. This was a treacherous landscape where an army could easily be cut off and, worst of all, lose its horses to starvation. The Mongol failure to recover from 'Ayn Jalut and press home their attack was perhaps a recognition that this was a hostile environment. Where the grasslands ran out, whether in eastern Europe or the Middle East, the Mongol advance stalled and failed.

Mongol campaigns in Asia *c.* 1300

- the Great Khanate, 1268
- conquered by the Great Khan (Kubilai Khan), 1268–79
- western khanates owing nominal allegiance to the Great Khan
- tributary to Mongol state

REPUBLIC OF NOVGOROD

KHANATE OF THE GOLDEN HORDE

- Bulgar
- Sarai
- Sarai

- Urgench
- Bukhara
- Tashkent
- Khodzhent
- Samarkand
- Kashgar
- Merv
- Khotan
- Kabul

CHAGATAI KHANATE

Aral Sea

Amu Darya

Syr Darya

Indus

GREAT KHANATE

- Karakorum

- Hsiliang

TIBET
1294 independent nominal Mongol overlords to 1368

- Lhasa

- Mirath 1329

SULTANATE OF DELHI
- Delhi

- Patna

Ganges

- Zhongdu
- K'ai-feng
- Hsian
- Nanjing
- Hangzhou
- Yangchou

Huang Ho

Yellow Sea

Sea of Japan

JAPAN

Kao-li

1274 and 1281

reinforcements 1281

East China Sea

Yangtze

Chang Jiang

- Dali
- Chongqing
- Wuchou
- Canton (Guangzhou)
- Fuchou
- Quanchou

Tropic of Cancer

Taiwan

1277–87

1278

1251

1285 Shenglong

Hainan 1281

- Gujerat
- Somnath

BURMA

Bengal

Bay of Bengal

- Pagan

KINGDOM OF PAGAN
- Pegu

ANNAM

KHMER EMPIRE
- Angkor

CHAMPA
- Vijaya

1292 unsuccessful expedition to Java

HINDU STATES
- Goa
- Calicut
- Madurai

Arabian Sea

Orissa

Ceylon

→ Kubilai Khan's campaigns, 1268–79
→ Kubilai Khan's campaigns, 1274–92
→ other Mongol campaign

CHAPTER SIX

THE VIKINGS

THE VIKING SHIP *was perfectly adapted to the needs of these hardy adventurers. Swift, with a draught shallow enough to enter rivers and creeks, it gave the Vikings the same advantage of mobility over their opponents and victims as the camels of the Bedouin and the ponies of the Turks did over theirs.*

THE VIKINGS

The geography of the Viking lands meant that sea travel was by far the easiest means of communication and the fjords of the Scandinavian coastlines provided excellent anchorages. Denmark, Sweden and Norway also lacked powerful rulers who could control Viking warriors.

THE NAME VIKINGS has an immediate resonance for most people in the English speaking world. Whereas the Huns, Arabs and Mongols seem to belong to the 'other', remote and inaccessible in both their culture and geographical location, the image of the Vikings is clear enough. They are part of the folk memory of western culture that has been handed down from generation to generation. And what an image it is: the Viking warrior, often with his horned helmet (for which, sadly, there is no real historical evidence) stands on the shore, sword in hand, his ship pulled up on the beach behind. There is probably a burning monastery in the background and booty being carried down to the ships. In fact, of course, the reality was much more complex: Vikings as farmers, Vikings as merchants, Vikings as explorers were just as typical as Vikings as pirates.

The origins of the name Viking are obscure but the Old Norse word meant 'fighting at sea' while the sea raider and robber was called a Viking. People of the Viking age used many different words, Northman (or Normans), Danes, or, further east among the Slavs, Rus, another name of obscure origin. For the historian of warfare, however, the term Viking conveniently describes the extraordinarily effective fighter who dominated the northern seas and the coastlands from the end of the eighth century until around 1066.

The Vikings were not in a strict sense nomads. Wanderers certainly, restless in their determination to seek new lands and sources of wealth. But they were also settlers: when they found good pasture and established homesteads, in France, Britain, Iceland or even distant Greenland, they set up home there, founding villages, trading centres and eventually churches. Of the other nomad peoples in

A replica Viking ship, under bare poles, lies in the lee of the Lofoten Islands in the north of Norway. The fjords, inlets and numerous islands of Scandinavia meant that boats were the only practical means of communication. Viking children must have learned to handle them from a very early age.

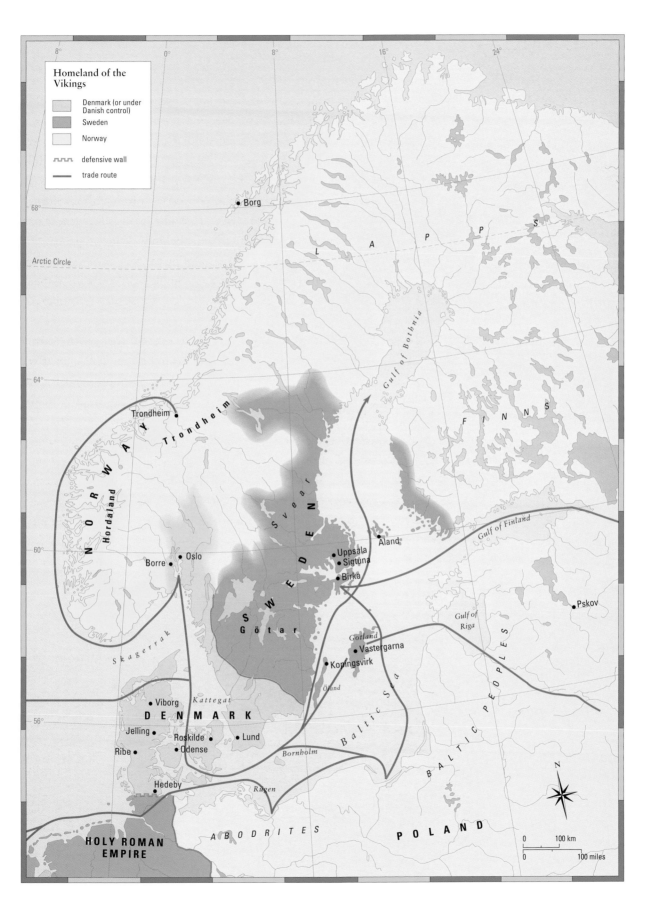

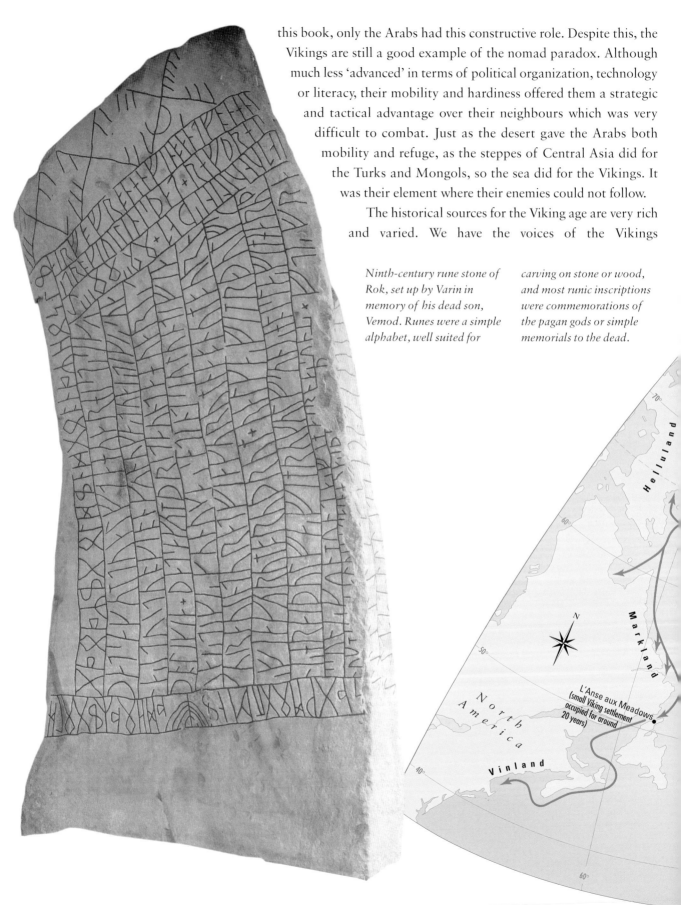

this book, only the Arabs had this constructive role. Despite this, the Vikings are still a good example of the nomad paradox. Although much less 'advanced' in terms of political organization, technology or literacy, their mobility and hardiness offered them a strategic and tactical advantage over their neighbours which was very difficult to combat. Just as the desert gave the Arabs both mobility and refuge, as the steppes of Central Asia did for the Turks and Mongols, so the sea did for the Vikings. It was their element where their enemies could not follow.

The historical sources for the Viking age are very rich and varied. We have the voices of the Vikings

Ninth-century rune stone of Rok, set up by Varin in memory of his dead son, Vemod. Runes were a simple alphabet, well suited for carving on stone or wood, and most runic inscriptions were commemorations of the pagan gods or simple memorials to the dead.

176

themselves, in their runes, which are usually simple inscriptions of names and invocations, and in their literature. There is a problem in that Viking literature was only written down after the Viking age had ended. With the coming of Christianity and literacy, we find Scandinavian antiquarians, like the great Snorri Sturluson at the beginning of the thirteenth century, collecting the material and recording it for posterity. It is from this period that the written versions of the sagas and the heroic poems, or *eddas*, date. The historian has to use them with caution because they have clearly been edited and both the details and even their spirit may have been changed to suit later ideas. Some sagas, such as the *Jomsviking Saga* about a group of freelance Viking adventurers, seem to be largely fiction, exciting and lurid but not historical evidence. On the other hand,

VIKING ROUTES TO NORTH AMERICA *c.* 1000

Viking expansion along the Atlantic seaways was a natural extension of their forays in the North Sea and the Baltic. Iceland and the west coast of Greenland were colonized and there was a short-lived outpost on the shores of Newfoundland.

Viking routes to
North America *c.* 1000

→ Norse voyages of exploration and settlement

▮ Norse settlement in Greenland

One of the ships excavated at Roskilde, Denmark, where the remains of five ships which had been used to block the entrance to the fjord have been recovered. The ship is made of oak and clinker-built around the central frame. The ships were light and supple, bending slightly to take the stress of wind and waves.

the *Orkneyinga Saga*, which, as its name suggests, deals with the fortunes of the Vikings of the Orkney Islands, has a strong basis in historical reality.

We have controls on this Viking literature from the numerous accounts of their raids and manners from their victims, the authors of the *Anglo-Saxon Chronicle*, the Frankish annalists of northern France or the Arabic historians of Muslim Spain. These give us dates and names, firmly anchored in historical fact, showing that we are not dealing with an imaginary heroic past. The Vikings are also the only one of the peoples discussed in this book who have left a substantial record in archaeology. They built fortresses and homesteads which have been excavated. In some cases trading centres like York and Dublin can be reconstructed in considerable detail. Many weapons and even textiles have survived in damp and peaty deposits and thus we have much more detailed information about Viking weapons than of other peoples of the early Middle Ages. Most astonishing is the survival of their ships, including the famous Oseberg ship from southern Norway and the group of different vessels from Roskilde in Denmark. Without these precious survivals, we would have no real idea how these great voyages were accomplished.

To understand the military success of the Vikings, we must turn first to their ships because it was these which gave them the technological advantage, the

Viking equivalent, so to speak, of the mounted archery of the steppe nomad. Viking ships came in many different shapes and sizes but there was a clear distinction between warships and cargo or trading ships. All Viking ships were clinker-built, with overlapping planks nailed on to a wooden framework. This style of shipbuilding became standard in northern Europe but it marked a major departure from the classical Mediterranean tradition of shipbuilding, where the planks were joined edge to edge by grooved joints and where there was no interior frame at all. The hulls were usually made of oak but pine was used for the masts and spars. The Viking method of building produced ships which were light and strong but also flexible, so that they could ride and bend with the seas. On the replica of the Gokstad ship, which was sailed across the Atlantic in 1893, it was noted that the keel would rise and fall by up to 2 cm (³/₄ inch) and the gunwales twist up to 15 cm (6 inches) out of true.

The warships were superbly designed for their function. These were the famous longships, often called *snekkja* in Viking times. These could be powered both by oars and sails. The oars enabled them to operate in confined

The Oseberg ship, dating from the ninth century, was excavated from the burial mound of a Norwegian princess. This ship was probably never used for warfare. The excellent preservation of the timbers allows us to appreciate the fine and elegant lines typical of Viking shipbuilding.

spaces or against the wind while sails made it possible for long voyages in the open sea to be undertaken. They were steered by a large oar attached on the starboard (that is, the steering-board) side to the stern. This steering-board projected below the level of the keel, to give it greater pull, but could be raised when the ship entered shallow waters. Ships would also have had iron anchors or anchors with iron flukes and wooden stocks. Fragments of anchor chains have also been found. These would allow ships to be moored away from land so the crew could rest, safe from their enemies. A reconstruction of one of the Roskilde ships has shown that it could make 9 knots under sail and 5 knots when being rowed, as fast as any vessels constructed before the age of steam. The reconstructed Gokstad ship reached 10 knots and more on its transatlantic voyage. These speeds suggest, in theory at least, that the crossing from western Denmark to eastern England could take less than forty-eight hours and

A Viking anchor. Crude but effective, it consists of a large rock between a forked branch and is held in place by a wooden post.

the passage from Norway to Iceland could be made in three days. Of course conditions would seldom have been ideal and most voyages would have taken longer, with ships struggling against the prevailing winds and being blown off course. The passage from Denmark to England might equally have taken four days' continuous rowing, or at least a week allowing for rest periods. Even so, these timings imply that it was not a very ambitious voyage and could be temptingly easy once news spread about the wealth of England and the lack of defences.

A second vital design feature was the very shallow draught of at least some of these ships. The same Roskilde ship had a draught of no more than 18 inches when fully laden. Because of the design of the hull and the keel, this seems to have been achieved without any loss of stability. It enabled them to bring their ships right up rivers such as the Loire, which were much too shallow and filled with sand-bars to allow more conventional navigation. They may also have been able to escape from pursuit by larger vessels by skimming through shallow waters.

As might be expected, the ships varied greatly in size. The small warship reconstructed on the basis of the Roskilde finds was 57 feet long and 8 feet wide. It carried a crew of twenty-six oarsmen and there may also have been a captain or steersman on board. Another of the Roskilde ships, not so well preserved, was much larger, probably just under 100 feet long and 13 feet wide. By analogy, it might have had spaces for fifty oarsmen. The Gokstad ship had spaces for sixteen oarsmen on each side and the coloured shields they attached to the outside of the boat were recovered in its excavation. In all these cases the numbers of oarsmen may have been supplemented by other warriors.

A replica Viking ship at sea. The ships were equally effective under sail or oars. This meant that long voyages could be made under wind power but that oars could be used for manoeuvring in narrow stretches of water. Naval battles were comparatively rare and, when they did occur, the ships were lashed together to form platforms for men to fight from.

Ships were often described according to the number of oarsmen they could hold. The smallest ships were so narrow that one man could hold two oars, one on each side. Larger ships were described by the number of benches they carried for two oarsmen. The standard ship specified in ship-levies was the twenty bencher, i.e. forty oarsmen, but ships of up to thirty benches are recorded.

We have an account, dating from around 1200, of the building of a great ship by Olaf Tryggvason, king of Norway, near Trondheim in 998.

Although the Bayeux Tapestry dates from the end of the eleventh century, after the Viking period, the illustrations of building ships for the invasion of England in 1066 give a vivid idea of the processes and skills involved. Here timbers are felled.

The winter after King Olaf came from Halogaland he had a great vessel built which was larger than any ship in the country and of which the frames can still be seen there. The keel that rested upon the grass was seventy-four ells [about 120 feet] long. Thorberg Skaffhog was the name of the man in charge of making the stem and stern of the vessel but there were many others, some to fell wood, some to shape it, some to make nails, some to carry timber. All that was used was very carefully chosen. The ship was long and broad and high-sided and strongly timbered. While they were planking the ship, it happened that Thorberg had to go home to his farm on urgent business and he stayed there a long time. The ship was planked up on both sides when he returned. That same evening the king went out with Thorberg to see how the vessel looked and everybody said that so large and beautiful a ship of war had never been seen before. Then the king returned to the town. Early next morning the king returned to the ship with Thorberg. The carpenters were standing doing nothing. The king asked them why they were doing that. They replied that the ship was spoilt and that somebody had gone from stem to stern and cut one deep notch after another down one side of the planking. When the king came nearer and saw that this was so, he immediately said that the man who had damaged the ship out of envy should die if he were found out, 'And the man who can tell me who it was will get great rewards from me.'

Then Thorberg said, 'I will tell you king who did it: I did it.'

The king replied: 'You must restore it to the same condition as before or you will pay for it with your life.'

Then Thorberg went and smoothed the ship's side until all the notches had disappeared. Then the king and all who were there declared that the ship was much handsomer on the side which Thorberg had cut, and the king asked him to shape it on both sides and gave him great thanks for the improvement. Afterwards Thorberg was the master-builder of the ship until she was finished. The ship was a dragon, built like the one the king had captured in Halogaland but this one was much larger and more carefully made in all her parts. The king called this ship *Long Serpent* and the other *Short Serpent*. The *Long Serpent* had thirty-four benches for rowers. The prow and the stern were covered in gilding and the freeboard was as great as in ocean-going ships. This ship was the best and most costly one ever built in Norway.

OVERLEAF: *No shipbuilding manuals survive from the Viking period but the Bayeux tapestry gives a clear idea of the tools and methods used in construction. Here timbers are planed, hulls are constructed and masts are set.*

The picture is fascinating. The great ship is built on the orders of the king. It is constructed on the grass and, apparently, completed in the winter. The shipbuilder is clearly highly skilled but he is also a farmer with other business to attend to. His relationship with the king seems to be one of easy familiarity but he clearly enjoys the respect of the workforce. The completed ship is the object of great popular admiration.

Navigation must have been based on long experience of watching the weather and the stars. The Vikings had no magnetic compass but latitude could be estimated from the positions of the stars and the existence of land could be deduced from the presence of birds or cloud formations, even if the land itself could not be seen. Even so, navigation on longer voyages across the open sea must have been very perilous. In contrast, sailing down the west coast of France and Spain, as they did in the great voyages of 843–60 and again in 966–71, must have been comparatively easy, if only from a navigational point of view.

We do not have many first-hand descriptions of naval warfare, in the sense of battles between fleets. When fleets did meet, the tactics seem to have been very conservative for such brilliant seamen. The ships were roped together to make a fighting platform and the two lines of battle met head-on. As they approached each other, showers of stones and arrows would be discharged. When the fleets finally clashed, the fighting would be hand-to-hand, like a land battle in the bows of the vessels, until one side proved victorious and started to take possession of the other's ships.

An important reason for the success of the Vikings was their access to raw materials. Timber, of course, was found in abundance and Viking ships were often made of high-quality oak. The other important raw material was iron, used for the nails which held their ships together. There were good supplies of bog iron in the Telemark area of southern Norway, at Dalarna in central Sweden and Smaland in the south. Compared with the people of the Mediterranean, where timber was always a problem, or the Indian Ocean where they sewed their boats together, the use of high-quality materials goes a long way to explaining the success of Viking shipbuilders.

Iron was also important for the making of swords. Swords were highly prized and famous swords were given names, 'Mail-biter' or 'Golden Hilt', for example, and they virtually acquired a personality of their own. Some swords were imported from France and the Rhineland but they were also made in Scandinavia itself. They were one-handed hacking swords, rather than thrusting weapons with both edges sharpened, measuring about 3 feet, including the short hilt. They were wielded with one hand, which must have required considerable strength, and carried not on belts around the waist but on shoulder straps. The hilts might be decorated with silver or gold ornaments. Scandinavian swords were actually exported along the Russian rivers to iron-poor areas such as the Muslim East where they commanded high prices for their hardness and flexibility.

Along with swords went iron-pointed spears which were used as thrusting weapons and smaller throwing javelins. Spearheads up to 2 feet long have been found and were mounted on shafts 6–9 feet long. Like swords, spears could sometimes be high-status weapons with silver ornamentation. Throwing javelins, which might easily be lost in battle, were of course much plainer. Bows do not seem to have played a major part in the Viking arsenal but one complete bow has been found, about 6 foot long and made of yew. It was very different from the short compound bows of the Central Asian nomads and must have been used by foot archers. Battleaxes, too, were certainly used but it is often difficult to tell whether an axe head was a weapon or simply a domestic tool: in some cases it may have been both. As late as 1203, when the French chronicler Villehardouin visited Constantinople, he remarked on the Varangian guard (of Viking origin) arrayed with their battleaxes ready to protect the emperor.

Viking shields were round and about a yard in diameter. They were usually made of wood with a circular metal boss in the centre with leather or metal bindings at the edges. They were frequently painted and writers comment on the brightly coloured shields which were arrayed along the edge of the fighting ships.

Viking warriors were in the main foot soldiers and the use of

ABOVE: *A Viking sword ceremonially bent as part of a burial ritual. It has a straight blade and measures about three foot, including the hilt. Viking swords were mostly one-handed hacking weapons. Famous swords were given names and their achievements celebrated in poetry and saga.*

The hilt was the only part of the sword which carried any decoration and high-status weapons such as these might be ornamented in silver or gold. Viking swords were highly prized and were exported to iron-poor areas as far away as the Middle East.

Bronze spearheads with ornamented silver hilts.

horses in battle was very rare. Raiding by sea, they had little space for horses or their food. The richer among them protected themselves with helmets and chain mail as well developed as anything else in the West but most Viking warriors must have made do with leather jerkins and much more simple equipment. In major confrontations they seem to have formed lines with a centre and two wings. The leader would be in the centre with his standard-bearer close by, both surrounded by a guard whose job it was to protect them. There seems to have been little refinement of tactics or mobility, both sides struggling with their opponents until one was overwhelmed and either broke or fled.

No one knows the reason for the Viking raids on the coastal areas of western Europe. They certainly took advantage of political instability and division in France, Britain and Ireland but such divisions were not new and in some ways the areas were stronger and better governed than they had been fifty or a hundred years previously. Explanations based on theories of over-population in the Viking lands again raise the question of why it became crucial at this particular time. It is possible too that developments in shipbuilding meant that longer-distance raids were possible for the first time; but if such improvements did take place, we have no idea what they were, for the classic Viking ships seem to be clearly derived from those of the pre-Viking age. The explanation may rather be that a small number of adventurers set out, were lucky and returned with enough booty to persuade others to follow their example, so that the whole process gathered momentum.

The first raids were small-scale and were conducted by groups of robbers and pirates without any central control. They were directed against coastal areas and up rivers by fleets of no more than ten or twelve ships and perhaps four or five hundred men. They did not attempt to occupy the land nor did they attempt to over-winter there.

The best evidence for the beginning of the raids comes from England where the *Anglo-Saxon Chronicle* gives us the fullest information. In about 789 three ships from Norway raided Portland on the Dorset coast and killed the local reeve. This seems to have been an isolated incident until 793 when Vikings raided and sacked the great monastery of Lindisfarne on the Northumbrian coast. The pillage of this great holy place made a profound impression for until then monasteries had usually been respected during periods of warfare. These people were clearly heathen barbarians. In 795 the first Viking raids on Ireland began

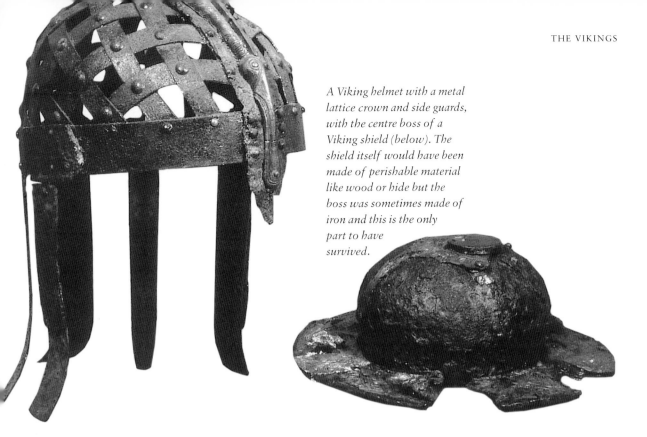

A Viking helmet with a metal lattice crown and side guards, with the centre boss of a Viking shield (below). The shield itself would have been made of perishable material like wood or hide but the boss was sometimes made of iron and this is the only part to have survived.

This crudely carved rune stone shows a Viking warrior on horseback armed with a sword and a round shield. The Vikings used their ships for transport but most fighting was done on land. The ships meant they could surprise the enemy, and also make a quick escape if the situation turned nasty.

and in 799 western France was hit for the first time. In these early years the Vikings did not have things all their own way. There was vigorous resistance on both sides of the Channel and both Charlemagne and the English kings erected fortifications to protect the coastline.

The division of the Carolingian Empire after 840, and the rivalries between the various princes, made France a much more attractive place to raid than England, where the local rulers continued to resist effectively. The problems had begun shortly beforehand when Dorestad, the main Frankish port on the lower Rhine, was sacked no less than three times between 834 and 837. In 843 a group of Vikings seized the island of Noirmoutier on the Atlantic coast of France, driving out the monks who had previously occupied it, and setting up a permanent base for further raids. By 858 they had established another base on the

Lindisfarne, or Holy Island, off the coast of Northumberland. The monastery on the island was one of the greatest centres of learning and spiritual life in early Anglo-Saxon England. Its sack by the Vikings in 793 caused widespread alarm and marked the beginning of more than two centuries of raids. Little remains of the monastery sacked by the Vikings. In the background we see the later medieval castle.

island of Oissel (in the Seine just upstream from Rouen) and the king, Charles the Bald, was unable to dislodge them because of an attack by his brother Lothar from the east.

The establishment of the base at Noirmoutier clearly fired the ambitions of the most adventurous Vikings. The very next year, 844, a fleet of about one hundred ships set off to the south. Their purpose seems less the fulfilment of a master plan; more, simply to discover what pickings could be had. The inhabitants of the north coast of Spain resisted fiercely, so they moved on to sack Lisbon and Cadiz before sailing up the Guadalquivir river to Seville. Here they met their match, for the Arab rulers of Spain had an efficient army and summoned help from all over their dominions. The Vikings were severely defeated and forced to flee back to the Loire.

VIKINGS IN THE MEDITERRANEAN 844, 859–62 AND 912–13

The Mediterranean offered rich hunting grounds for the Vikings. While the Arabic states of North Africa were able to repel the raiders, France and Italy suffered badly. In the east the Vikings reached the Black Sea via the Dnepr, which allowed them to raid the riches of the Byzantine Empire and Persia.

In 859 one of the most spectacular of all raids began. Hastein and Bjorn Ironsides led sixty-two ships south. They were driven off from the west coast of Spain but sailed through the Straits of Gibraltar; finding less formidable defences they raided the east coast of Spain and the Balearic islands. Over the winter of 859–60 they established themselves in the Camargue and raided France up the Rhône valley. Sailing east in the spring they destroyed the city of Luna in northern Italy (which they thought was Rome) and Pisa and Fiesole just outside Florence. In 861 they returned, again being driven off by the Spanish Muslims but sacking the Basque capital at Pamplona on the way home. Only twenty of the original ships

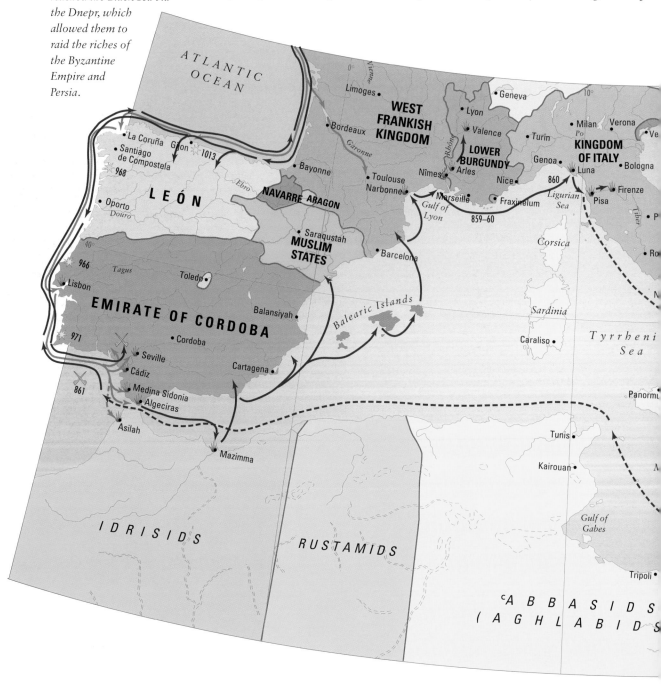

returned. The expedition was the boldest and most far-reaching Viking foray into the Mediterranean but it was no campaign of conquest. The Vikings were raiders and booty collectors who relied on speed and surprise to achieve their ends. Faced by real resistance, they soon left to look for softer targets.

During the 860s France offered a less easy prey. Charles the Bald employed a mixture of military force and the payment of Danegeld (massive amounts of silver) to keep the Vikings at bay. In the Loire area, the local counts destroyed the Viking bases and drove them out; and in 866 the Vikings, loaded with bribes, left the Seine.

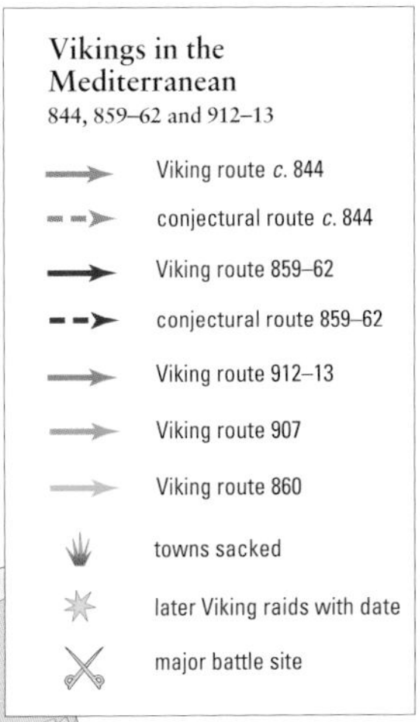

Vikings in the Mediterranean
844, 859–62 and 912–13

Viking route c. 844
conjectural route c. 844
Viking route 859–62
conjectural route 859–62
Viking route 912–13
Viking route 907
Viking route 860
towns sacked
later Viking raids with date
major battle site

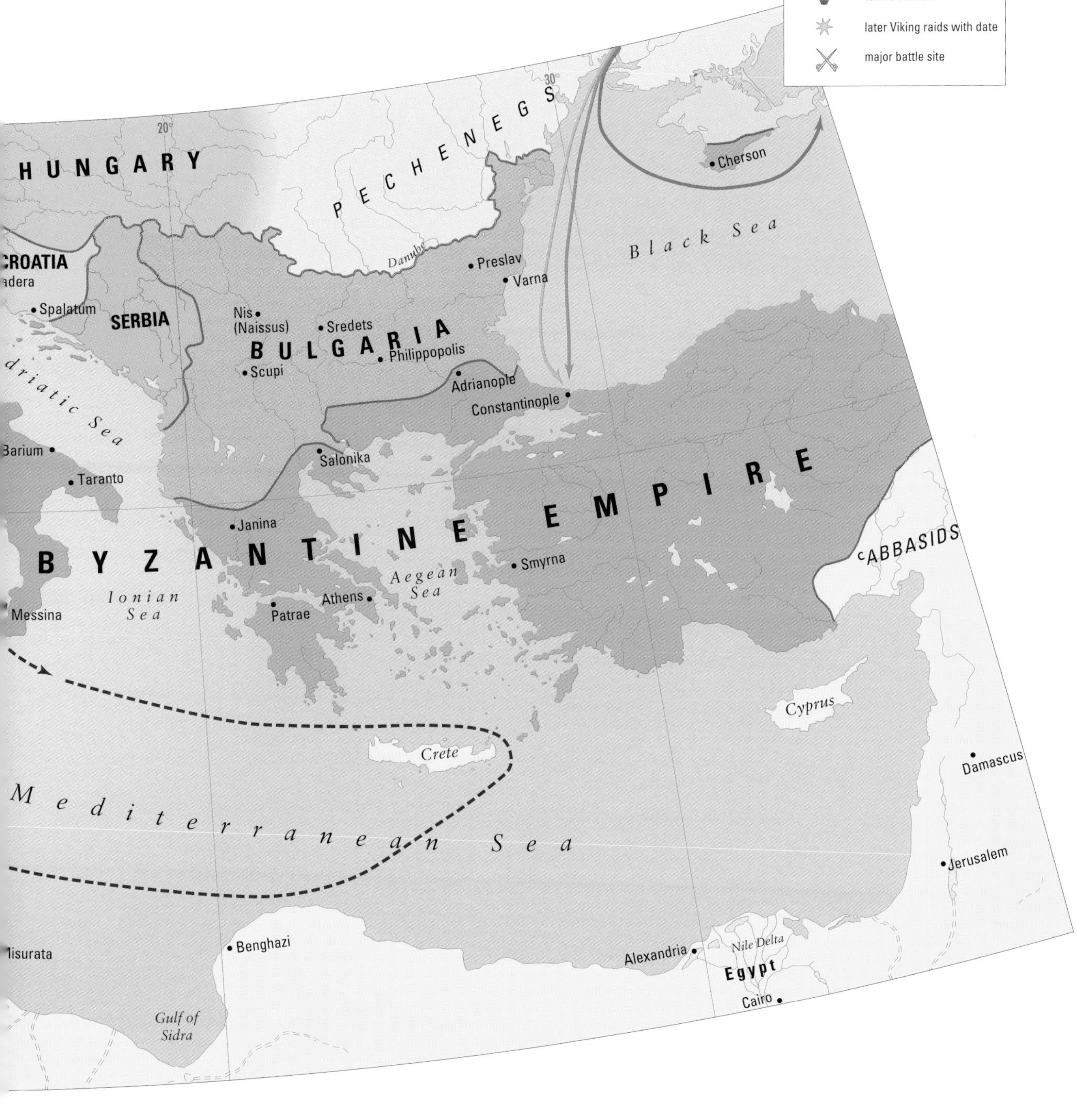

The respite given to France was a result of events across the Channel. In 865 two Viking leaders, Ivar and Halfdan, led a great army from Denmark to attack East Anglia. This was much more than a raid. The army intended to come and to stay. The kings of East Anglia paid them in horses to go away and they set off north. In 866 they took York and within a decade they had established it as the centre of a Viking kingdom. In 869 they defeated and killed Edmund, the last king of East Anglia and that, too, was incorporated into what became known as the Danelaw. In 873 the army attacked Mercia and took the capital at Repton: the last king of Mercia fled to Rome and the kingdom was incorporated in the Viking lands. Only Wessex, where Alfred mounted a spirited resistance, was able to hold out. The Danes had begun their invasion as a massive army bent on slaughter and plunder, but after a decade the character of their presence had changed greatly. Many of them had now settled down, possessing land and becoming farmers. In York they established a major trading post outside the walls of the Roman city. The Viking kingdom was more peaceful and its inhabitants were no longer brigands and pirates.

Comparative stability in England persuaded Vikings who wanted adventure and plunder to turn their attention again to France. From 878 to 885 a Viking army moved through northern France, choosing a different base every winter and using the summers to sack and pillage. Having destroyed Flanders and the Rhineland, they moved up the Seine in 885 and attacked Paris, then still a fairly small city on the island in the river. Under the leadership of Count Odo, the Parisians put up a heroic resistance, described in an account of the siege written by Abbon who describes how the Vikings for the first time mastered the art of using siege engines against the walls. Despite this, the defence held out until the king, Charles the Fat, arrived. Paris was saved but the rest of France continued to suffer from the raiders. In 889 Count Odo drove them from the Seine valley. Fortresses and town walls were now appearing all over northern France and, once again, the Vikings looked across the Channel for easier pickings. In 911 King Charles the Simple of France made a treaty with Rollo, last of the Viking leaders in the country. Rollo and his followers were granted the area ever since known as Normandy (Northman's land) for settlement. In exchange, Rollo and his men were to act as guardians of the land against their fellows. It was effectively the end of Viking attacks on France.

In England, a much more conventional pattern of warfare between Wessex and the Vikings was now emerging. The days of swift raids and evacuations had passed and the Anglo-Saxons were proving a good military match for their enemies. Soon they were able to take the initiative and between 909 and 917 Edward the Elder was able to reconquer the Danelaw south of the Humber, leaving the Vikings to rule York and the north-east. Meanwhile Vikings had established themselves in the north and west of Scotland, making Orkney, Shetland and Caithness their homelands and dominating the western seas around the Hebrides. In Ireland, too, they took advantage of the divisions among the

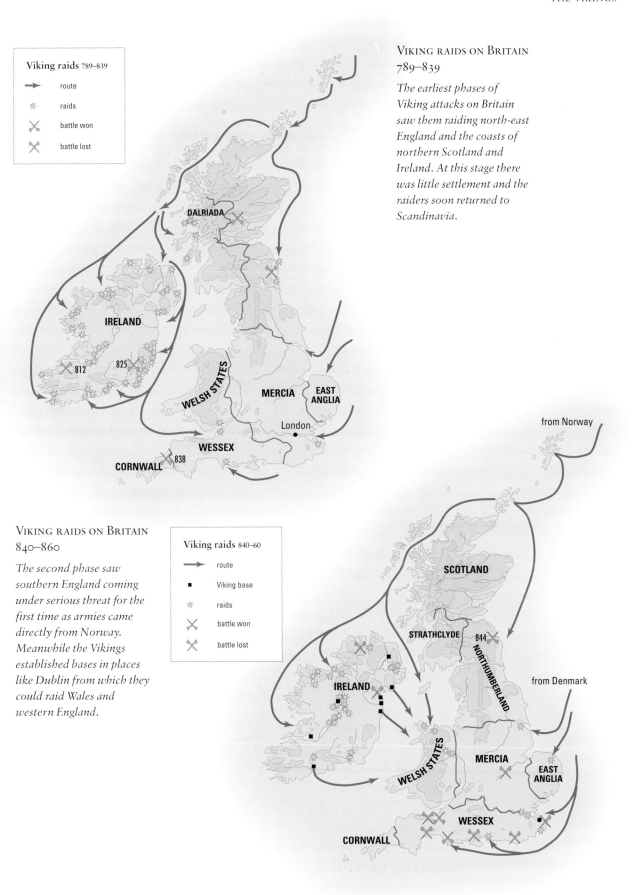

Viking raids 789–839

→ route
✳ raids
✕ battle won
✕ battle lost

VIKING RAIDS ON BRITAIN 789–839

The earliest phases of Viking attacks on Britain saw them raiding north-east England and the coasts of northern Scotland and Ireland. At this stage there was little settlement and the raiders soon returned to Scandinavia.

DALRIADA

IRELAND

812

825

WELSH STATES

MERCIA

EAST ANGLIA

London

WESSEX

CORNWALL 838

from Norway

VIKING RAIDS ON BRITAIN 840–860

The second phase saw southern England coming under serious threat for the first time as armies came directly from Norway. Meanwhile the Vikings established bases in places like Dublin from which they could raid Wales and western England.

Viking raids 840–60

→ route
■ Viking base
✳ raids
✕ battle won
✕ battle lost

SCOTLAND

STRATHCLYDE

844

NORTHUMBERLAND

from Denmark

IRELAND

WELSH STATES

MERCIA

EAST ANGLIA

WESSEX

CORNWALL

DANISH GREAT ARMY
865–79

The great Danish army based itself in England, destroying the kingdom of East Anglia and raiding deep into Wessex and wintering at Repton. York now became a permanent Viking base and trading centre and the Danelaw became virtually an independent state.

Danish Great Army
865–879

■ Viking base

← campaigns of the Great Army 865–73

extent of Danelaw

✕ battle won

✕ battle lost

other areas under Viking rule

fluctuating Viking control

Shetland Isles
to Norway

Orkney

EARLDOM OF ORKNEY

SCOTLAND

North Sea

NORTHUMBERLAND

STRATHCLYDE

KINGDOM OF YORK

York

Torksey

Isle of Man

Irish Sea

IRELAND

Dublin

Nottingham

Repton

EAST ANGLIA

Limerick

Thetford

WELSH STATES

ENGLISH MERCIA

DANISH MERCIA

Wexford

Waterford

Cork

Gloucester

Cirencester

London

Chippenham

Reading

W E S S E X

Exeter

Wareham

English Channel

WEST FRANKISH KINGDOM

Viking campaigns
878–900

The final stage of Viking campaigns in England saw the complete conquest of the country by Cnut. England now became part of a North Sea empire which incorporated Denmark and much of southern Scandinavia. On the other side of the Channel, the Vikings established the Duchy of Normandy from 911.

Shetland Isles to Norway

Viking campaigns
878–900

- 878–92
- 893
- 894–5
- Viking base
- Danelaw
- other areas under Viking rule
- fluctuating Viking control
- battle lost
- English burh

Orkney

EARLDOM OF ORKNEY

SCOTLAND

North Sea

STRATHCLYDE

NORTHUMBERLAND

KINGDOM OF YORK
York

IRELAND
Dublin
Limerick
Wexford
Waterford
Cork

Irish Sea

Isle of Man

Chester
Buttington
Bridgenorth

DANISH MERCIA

EAST ANGLIA

878–84

WELSH STATES

ENGLISH MERCIA

Lea
Benfleet
Shoebury
London
Thorney
Fulham River
Milton

Pilton

WESSEX

Lymne

Boulogne 892

Exeter

884–85
Amiens

English Channel

from Nantes 892

WEST FRANKISH KINGDOM

197

The wealth of the Vikings can be seen in this hoard of coins and metalwork found at Cuerdale in Lancashire, England. Probably buried by Vikings driven out of Dublin in 902, it comprised over 8,000 objects, many of them silver coins from as far away as Muslim Central Asia. Whether this was booty, or the profits of legitimate trade, we shall never know.

Irish kingdoms to raid deep into the country up the rivers. They established a precarious kingdom based on Dublin which, like York, became a major trading post. But Irish resistance was vigorous and many Norsemen went looking for richer gains elsewhere. When Brian Boru, king of Munster, defeated them at the battle of Clontarf in 1015 (though he himself died in the conflict) Viking power in the island effectively came to an end.

It was not until the end of the tenth century that Viking armies attacked England again. This time they were not individuals or groups of raiders acting on their own initiative but organized armies, led at first by Olaf Tryggvason of Norway and later by Svein and his son Cnut, kings of Denmark. They all hoped to use the wealth of England to establish their authority in their home kingdoms and indeed Cnut ended by making England, not his native Denmark, the real centre of power. In 991 Olaf defeated the East Anglians under the ealdorman Byhrtnoth at Maldon in Essex, a defeat commemorated in one of the greatest Anglo-Saxon poems. Olaf's triumph enabled him to return to Norway with a massive 22,000 pounds of silver and establish himself as king (and build, as we have seen, the great ship, *Long Serpent*). Other rulers saw the easy pickings which were to be had from England under the feeble rule of Ethelred, nicknamed the 'Unready' (which actually means badly advised).

The new enemy was Svein Forkbeard of Denmark, who had first raided England as an ally of Olaf of Norway. He attacked again in 1007, at first merely taking Danegeld and then returning home. By 1013, however, he seems to have decided on a policy of the conquest of the whole kingdom. In this he was aided by many Anglo-Saxons, who felt that his strong rule would be preferable to the chaos they were currently enduring. Svein died in 1013 and was succeeded by Cnut who had himself crowned and who turned out to be one of England's greatest kings. But by this time he and his men could hardly be described as Vikings. Rather, he was a Christian monarch with a strong army, a chancery and all the trappings of settled government: the Viking age was over.

Heroic memories and ideals lived on and we will leave the Vikings with the heroic image of Cnut's fleet setting out for England:

The end of the Viking age was marked by the conversion of the Vikings to Christianity and the assertion of royal power over unruly subjects. By the eleventh century Denmark and Norway were conventional kingdoms much like others in Western Europe. The growing power of the kings can be seen in this massive fortress in Denmark built by Cnut, who was also king of England.

A Viking warship as illustrated in an Anglo-Saxon manuscript of c. 1025–50. While it is clearly not realistic, we can see the planking and the nails as well as the steering oars and the splendid figurehead. The structure in the centre by the mast may represent some sort of cabin or shelter.

The king Cnut, bidding his mother and brother farewell, again sought the bounds of the encircling shore where he had gathered a brilliant show of two hundred ships. Indeed there was so great a supply of arms that a single one of those ships could have furnished weapons in the greatest abundance if all the rest had lacked them. For there were so many types of shields that you would have thought that the hosts of all nations were at hand. Further, there was such elegant decoration on the keels that to the dazzled eyes of observers viewing from a distance, they seemed to be made of flame rather than of wood. For if at any time the sun mingled with them the radiance of its beams, here would flash the glitter of armour, there the fire of the hanging shields; burning gold on the prows, gleaming silver in the varied decorations of the vessels ... What adversary could gaze upon the lions,

Ships at sea, from the Bayeux Tapestry. The ships are being swept along by a favourable breeze and there is no sign that oars are being used except for steering. We see the multicoloured shields arrayed along the sides of the ships, the sails and the figureheads. Note also that some of the ships were large enough to carry horses.

terrible in the glitter of their gold, upon the men of metal, menacing with their gilded brows, upon the dragons flaming with refined gold, upon the bulls threatening slaughter, their horns gleaming with gold – all these on the ships – and not feel dread and fear in the face of a king with so great a fighting force? Moreover, in this great armada, none among them was a slave, none a freed-man, none of low birth, none enfeebled by age. All were noble, all strong in the power of maturity, all fully trained in any type of warfare, all of such fleetness that they despised the speed of cavalry.

This was perhaps the high point of the seaborne armies that had conquered and ravaged much of western Europe for two centuries; but their weaknesses were to be cruelly exposed by the mailed Norman knights at Hastings in 1066.

THE END OF NOMAD DOMINANCE

A Bedouin tribesman leads his camel past a ruined column in the ancient city of Petra, Jordan. In reality, the Arab conquests were much less destructive than the Mongol invasions and city life continued to thrive in the Middle East throughout the early MiddleAges at a time when it was almost extinct in the West.

THE END OF NOMAD DOMINANCE

THE END OF THE Mongol expansion did not mean the end of the military achievements of nomad peoples but the tide gradually began to turn against them. Tamerlane (d. 1405) was in some ways a nomad conqueror, and presented himself as a successor of Genghis Khan, but his military forces were more like a traditional Middle Eastern military than a truly nomad army. Several milestones mark the decline of nomad predominance: the battle of Kulikovo Pole in 1380 when the Moscovites first defeated the Mongols of the Golden Horde, although it was not until the fall of Kazan to the troops of Ivan IV in 1552 that the triumph

Tamerlane invades India, from a fifteenth-century Persian manuscript. His forces, advancing from the right, are confronted by Indian horsemen and a formidable array of elephants. In fact, Tamerlane raided India but did not stay. Like Genghis Khan before him, he found that the heat and lack of good grazing did not suit his nomad followers at all.

Ivan IV, surnamed the Terrible, tsar 1533–84. His capture of Kazan in 1552 marked the end of the power of the Mongols in Russia. From this time on Russian forces slowly pushed south and east at the expense of the nomads until, with the crushing of the Tekke Turkmen in the 1880s, the nomads had been thoroughly tamed.

of the settled people was finally consolidated. In 1514 the Ottomans, using all the resources of a settled state, defeated the Safavid rulers of Iran, who still depended on a semi-nomad Turkmen military. More than anything else, it was the increasing range and mobility of gunpowder weapons which shifted the balance, for such weapons could only be produced in settled and organized societies. The forging of cannon and the making of handguns required advanced technologies, and established and stationary factories. Large and heavy quantities of fuel and water were necessary for forging the metal. The storage of gunpowder

The Victory Scroll *depicts the destruction of the Mongol fleet attacking Japan in 1281. The storm which destroyed the Mongol fleet was believed by the Japanese to be a sign of divine support, and certainly the only major attempt the Mongols made to launch a maritime campaign ended in disaster for them.*

required stone-built magazines. None of these were available in the nomad camp.

The bow maker by contrast, could work in the nomad tents; the wood, sinews and animal glues he required could all be found locally and transported easily when the camp moved. As long as the bow and the mounted archer remained the cutting edge of military technology, the nomad warriors would be able to terrorize and sometimes dominate more advanced settled peoples.

The development of gunpowder weapons enabled settled peoples to defend themselves against the attacks of nomads (at least if they were used effectively).

It did not, however, allow them to dominate the nomads in their home territories. The same obstacles to mobility still remained; indeed, in some ways they were made worse by the need to transport cannon and ammunition. Armies still moved very slowly and needed regular supplies of water and food. In traditional nomad environments, the tribesmen still had the upper hand. Desert Arabia was dominated by nomads until well into the twentieth century. The Saudi states, both the first one in the eighteenth century and the second one at the end of the nineteenth and the beginning of the twentieth, were founded by armies of puritanical Bedouin warriors. The Ottomans were obliged to pay them handsome subsidies to allow the pilgrimage caravans to make their way from Damascus and Cairo to the holy cities of Mecca and Medina through nomad territory. One of the reasons why the Bedouin were so happy to help T. E. Lawrence destroy the Hijaz railway was that they realized that the train could put an end to this lucrative business.

In southern Sudan the armies of the Mahdi who killed General Gordon in Khartoum in 1885 were largely nomads. The subsequent defeat of the Mahdi and his followers at Omdurman showed that they were a spent military force. In the deep Sahara the Tuareg and other nomad groups remained lords of their own domains until the expansion of French colonial power in the late nineteenth and early twentieth centuries. In Iran the transhumant Bakhtiari and Qashqai nomads of the Zagros mountains remained effectively free from government control until the time of Reza Shah in the 1920s and 1930s and in some areas until the 1950s. The last truly nomad group to dominate its settled neighbours militarily were the Tekke Turkmen of the Merv oasis in Turkmenistan, who were still raiding north-eastern Iran for slaves in the late nineteenth century and whose power was not finally broken until the Russians defeated them at Geok Tepe in 1881.

It was not so much new military technologies as new forms of transport that spelt the end of nomad independence in their own territories. In some cases the new technology was represented by the railways: the Turkmen of Central Asia

were subdued from the 1880s onwards by the Transcaspian railway, which meant that Russian troops could speedily be transported into their desert fastnesses. In Arabia it was the coming of the motor vehicle which cost the Bedouin their advantage of mobility. After the First World War, the British and French mandate powers in Iraq and Syria began to use air power to reach the Bedouin in the most inhospitable and remote parts of their territory. By the end of the twentieth century, nomad populations wielded no more than a shadow of their previous power. In a few countries like Jordan and Saudi Arabia, tribal chiefs were still a political power in the land; in remote areas of Yemen, the central government remained (and remains) so weak that nomads can still defy its authority, to an extent maintaining their own small armies and kidnapping foreigners to demand concessions from the administration in Sana'a. But these are no more than distant and faint echoes of a time when settled peoples from Western Europe to the South China Sea trembled at the threat of nomad attack.

A Central Asian nomad group moving camp. The wooden form of a yurt can be seen on the lead animal. The nomadic life still survives in many areas of North Africa, the Middle East and Central Asia, but the days when they could dominate and terrorize the settled populations have long since passed.

BIOGRAPHIES

ABU BAKR, CALIPH 632–4
One of Muhammad's earliest followers, he came
from a prominent Mecca family. He led the Muslim
community in the crucial two years after
Muhammad's death when the Muslims asserted
their control over the Arabian peninsula.

**AETIUS, FLAVIUS, MAGISTER MILITUM OF THE
WESTERN ROMAN EMPIRE**
From 425 to 454 he was the most important military
leader in the Roman West. He had been a hostage at
the Hunnic court and spoke the language. He used
the support of the Huns against his rival Boniface
and, in the 430s and 440s, to control Gaul. In 451
Attila attacked Gaul but was defeated by Aetius,
now allied with the Visigoths at the battle of the
Catalaunian Plains. Aetius was murdered by the
jealous Emperor Valentinian III in 454.

ALP ARSLAN, SELJUK SULTAN 1063–72
He consolidated Seljuk rule over Iran and the Fertile
Crescent with the aid of his Iranian minister Nizam
al-Mulk. In 1071 he led the Turkish army which
defeated the Byzantines at the battle of Manzikert.

'AMR B. AL-'AS (d. 664)
From the aristocratic Quraysh tribe in Mecca and
closely related to the Umayyads. In 641 he led the
Muslim invasion of Egypt and served as governor
there until 645 when he was dismissed by the caliph
Uthman who wanted a more compliant figure. In
658 he reconquered Egypt for the Umayyads and
remained governor until his death in 664.

ATTILA, KING OF THE HUNS 434–53
Reigned initially with his brother Bleda whom he
had murdered in 445 when he became sole ruler.
In the 440s he dominated the Balkans but in 451
turned his attention to Gaul. He was defeated in 451
at the battle of the Catalaunian Plains but led an

invasion of northern Italy the following year. He
died in his bed in 453.

**BATU, SON OF JUCHI, THE SON OF GENGHIS KHAN
(d. 1256)**
Mongol prince who was Subedei's partner in the
great expeditions against Russia in 1237–40 and
eastern Europe in 1241. Returned to the Volga
steppes where he and his Mongol followers formed
the Golden Horde.

BAYBARS, MAMELUKE SULTAN OF EGYPT 1260–77
One of the greatest soldiers of his age and a master
of siege warfare, he was second in command to
Sultan Kutuz when the Mamelukes defeated the
Mongols at 'Ayn Jalut in 1260. As sultan in his own
right, he played a major role in the destruction of
the remaining Crusader castles in the east, taking
Safed in 1266 and Crac des Chevaliers in 1271.

BELA IV, KING OF HUNGARY 1235–70
Early in his reign he was faced by the invasion of the
Mongols under Subedei and Batu and his own
barons' unwillingness to support him against the
invaders. He was defeated at Mohi in 1241 and
forced to flee to Croatia. When the Mongols left
later the same year, he returned to his kingdom and
spent the rest of his long reign repairing the damage.

**CHARLES THE BALD, KING OF THE WESTERN FRANKS
843–77**
Son of Louis the Pious and grandson of
Charlemagne. He attempted to organize the
defences of France against the Vikings but with
limited success, since they continued to raid the
Paris basin and the Loire Valley. He also resorted to
paying them large sums of money. After 865 many
Vikings went to England to join the Great Army
and as a result France enjoyed some respite for the
rest of his reign.

CHARLES THE SIMPLE, KING OF THE WESTERN FRANKS 898–923

The last of Charlemagne's descendants to rule in France, he was an unsuccessful monarch. In 911 he made the Treaty of St Clair-sur-Epte with the Viking Rollo, which granted Normandy to Rollo in exchange for protection against other Viking raiders.

CNUT, KING OF DENMARK 1013–35, AND ENGLAND 1017–35

He participated in his father Svein Forkbeard's invasions of England. On the death of Edmund of Wessex in November 1016 he was peacefully accepted as king of England. Since he also ruled Denmark and, for a time Norway, he created a North Sea empire and was one of the most powerful monarchs in Europe. In 1027 he made a famous pilgrimage to Rome.

EDMUND, KING OF EAST ANGLIA 856–69

The last of the Saxon kings of East Anglia, he was killed by the Viking Great Army in battle near Hoxne in Suffolk, probably on 20 November. He was later regarded as a saint and martyr and his tomb, at Bury St Edmunds, became the site of an important monastery.

EDWARD THE ELDER, KING OF WESSEX 899–924

Succeeded his father Alfred the Great. He continued the offensive against the Danes in eastern England. He also continued his father's policy of building fortified towns or *burh*s to contain the enemy. By 920 he had established his control over all of England south of the Humber and his reign marks the apogee of the Anglo-Saxon kingdom of Wessex.

FREDERICK II, HOLY ROMAN EMPEROR 1212–50

He was aware of the Mongol menace but his constant quarrels with the Papacy, which led to his formal (but not actual) deposition at the Council of Lyon in 1245, meant that he was unable to offer any real leadership in the struggle against the invaders.

HENRY THE PIOUS, DUKE OF SILESIA AND CRACOW 1238–41

Succeeded his ambitious father Henry the Bearded as the most powerful Polish magnate of his time. He was defeated by the Mongol army under Kadan and Baidar at Liegnitz on 9 April 1241 and killed while trying to escape.

HERACLIUS, BYZANTINE EMPEROR 610–41

Achieved power by military coup from North Africa. He led the Byzantine counter-attack against the Persians who had conquered most of the Middle East. In 628 he took and burned the Persian capital at Ctesiphon near Baghdad. In 636 his armies were defeated in Syria by the Muslims and the Middle East was once more lost to the Byzantine Empire.

HÜLEGÜ, SON OF TOLUI, THE SON OF GENGHIS KHAN (d. 1265)

In 1251 he was appointed to lead a new Mongol expedition to Iran, when his brother Kubilai was sent to China. He arrived in Iran 1256 and besieged and took the Assassin castles in the north. In 1258 he sacked Baghdad and executed the last Abbasid caliph. In 1260 he took Aleppo but left Syria to help choose a successor to the Great Khan. After his departure his deputy Kit-Buga was defeated by the Mamelukes at 'Ayn Jalut. Hülegü's descendants ruled Iran as Il-Khans until 1335.

AL-JAHIZ (d. 868)

Arab essayist who composed, among many other works, a treatise on the 'Virtues of the Turks' which is one of our main sources for the military nature of the Turks when they first arrived in the Middle East.

JALAL AL-DIN MENGUBIRTI (d. 1231)

Son of the last Khwarazm Shah. Unlike his father, he was a bold military commander who led guerrilla resistance to the Mongols throughout Iran. He was the only Persian commander who proved able to defeat them. He was finally cornered in eastern Turkey and killed by some Kurds in a cave in the mountains. With his death, organized resistance to the Mongols in Iran virtually ceased.

JUVAYNI (d. 1283)

Persian bureaucrat and historian who worked for the Mongol rulers of Iran. His account of the Mongol invasions of his homeland is one of our main sources for the period.

KHALID B. AL-WALID (d. 642)

A Meccan aristocrat who was one of the boldest and most successful of early Muslim generals. He made his reputation in the conquest of Arabia after Muhammad's death in 632. He then joined the campaign in Iraq but he was transferred to Syria where he played a leading role in the defeat of the Byzantines at the battle of the Yarmuk in 636. On being dismissed by the jealous caliph, he lived the rest of his life in comparative obscurity.

KHUSRAW II PARVIZ, SASANIAN SHAH OF IRAN 590–628

At his succession he was challenged by a rival, Bahram, but was reinstated with the aid of the Byzantine emperor Maurice in 591. On Maurice's murder in 602 he led a major invasion of the Roman east, conquering Syria, most of Turkey and Egypt. However, he was defeated by the Emperor Heraclius and was deposed and murdered by his own subjects. After his death, the Sasanian Empire descended into chaos.

KHWARAZM SHAH ('ALA AL-DIN) 1200–20

From the family of the hereditary rulers of Khwarazm (at the south end of the Aral Sea, Uzbekistan) he became ruler of most of eastern Iran. His arrogance, military incompetence and outright cowardice meant that he failed to co-ordinate any resistance to the Mongols. He fled and finally died taking refuge on an island in the Caspian Sea. It was left to his son Jalal al-Din to continue the struggle.

KUBILAI, SON OF TOLUI, THE SON OF GENGHIS KHAN

He was sent to China in 1260 when his brother Hülegü was sent to Iran. Here he engaged in a prolonged conflict with the Sung rulers of southern China which resulted in the subjugation of the whole country by 1279. He also succeeded his brother Mongke as Great Khan in 1259. Kubilai died in 1294 but his descendants ruled China from their new capital at Beijing until 1368.

MALIK SHAH, SON OF ALP ARSLAN, SELJUK SULTAN 1072–92

Greatest of the Seljuk rulers of Iran and the Fertile Crescent, his reign was a period of comparative peace and prosperity. Nizam al-Mulk (d. 1092), his vizier, wrote the *Book of Government*, which gives the best account of the training of Turkish soldiers.

AL-MA'MUN, 'ABBASID CALIPH 813–33

Began his reign in north-east Iran but defeated his brother to take over Baghdad and the west as well. A great patron of learning, it was in his reign that Turkish troops began to be employed in large numbers by the caliphs.

MONGKE, SON OF TOLUI THE SON OF GENGHIS KHAN, GREAT KHAN 1251–9

At his accession his brothers were despatched on expeditions to extend the Mongol Empire, Hülegü to Iran and Kubilai to China.

MUHAMMAD, THE PROPHET OF ALLAH (*c.* 570–632)

Born in Mecca, he began to receive the first revelations in about 600. In 622 he was obliged to flee with a few followers to Medina where he set up a small state which was the first Muslim community. In 630 he reconquered his home town of Mecca and established it as the centre of Muslim worship.

AL-MU'TASIM, 'ABBASID CALIPH 833–44

Succeeded his brother al-Ma'mun. He was the effective creator of the Turkish army which came to form the bulk of the armies of the caliphate.

NIZAM AL-MULK (d. 1092)
Persian vizier to the Seljuk Sultans Alp Arslan and Malik Shah. His *Book of Government* is our principal source of information about the training of Turkish soldiers.

OGEDEI, SON OF GENGHIS KHAN. GREAT KHAN 1227–41
Under his rule, the Mongol expeditions were sent to Russia and eastern Europe, although he played no part in the campaigns himself.

OLAF TRYGGVASON, KING OF NORWAY *c.* 995–100
Leader of the Viking invasions of England in 991 and 994. Whilst king of Norway he was responsible for the forced conversion of his country to Christianity.

RASHID AL-DIN, FADL ALLAH (d. 1318)
Physician and vizier to the Il-khanid (Mongol) rulers of Iran. Writer of a great *World History* which preserves old Mongol accounts of Genghis Khan's reign. Illustrated manuscripts of this work give a vivid picture of military costume and equipment at this time.

ROLLO, LORD OF NORMANDY 911 to *c.* 933
Probably of Norwegian origin, he was the leader of the Vikings in northern France. In 911 he signed the treaty of St Clair-sur-Epte with Charles the Simple (898–923) which granted him the area that later became the duchy of Normandy. He was the direct ancestor of William the Conqueror and all subsequent English monarchs.

ROMANUS IV DIOGENES, BYZANTINE EMPEROR 1068–71
Coming from a military background, he led several campaigns to contain Turkish expansion in Asia Minor. Defeated by the Seljuk sultan Alp Arslan at Manzikert in August 1071, he was well treated by the sultan but was subsequently deposed and murdered by Byzantine rivals.

SA'D B. ABI WAQQAS (d. *c.* 670)
A companion of the Prophet Muhammad from Mecca. He commanded the Muslim armies at the battle of Qadisiya in 636 when they defeated the Persian army and conquered Iraq. His subsequent career as governor of Iraq was less successful and he was accused of arrogance and corruption. He died in obscurity in Arabia in about 670.

SUBEDEI, MONGOL GENERAL (*c.* 1190–1242)
Said to have been the son of a blacksmith, his military talents led to rapid promotion in the armies of Genghis Khan. In 1217 he led the campaign against the Merkits, the last of Genghis's rivals among the Mongols. In 1220 he was active in the conquests in north-east Iran and led the pursuit of the Khwarazm Shah. From 1237 to 1241 he and Batu led the Mongol conquests of Russia and Eastern Europe.

THEODOSIUS II, EASTERN ROMAN EMPEROR 408–50
Succeeding as a boy of 7, he was of a scholarly and retiring disposition, being more interested in education and legal reforms than warfare. His reign was marked by almost continuous warfare with the Persians in the east and the Huns in the Balkans but he left military power in the hands of Gothic generals like Aspar and never took the field himself.

'UMAR B. AL-KHATTAB, CALIPH 634–44
He succeeded the first caliph Abu Bakr. He had a reputation for stern incorruptibility and his government became a model for future generations. Although never leading them in person, it was during his reign that the Muslim armies took Syria, Iraq and Egypt. Assassinated in Kufa (Iraq) in 644.

VALENTINIAN III, WESTERN ROMAN EMPEROR 425–55
Succeeding as a 6-year-old boy, he was dominated by his powerful mother Galla Placidia and generals like Boniface (killed 432) and Aetius (killed 454). The emperor was both weak and vicious and his assassination of the great Aetius in 454 sealed his own fate, for he was soon killed by Aetius' men.

FURTHER READING

The best introduction to the Huns is E. A. Thompson's *The Huns*, which should be consulted in the revised edition by Peter Heather (Oxford University Press, 1996). There is a good general account of the Huns and other barbarian invaders of the Roman Empire in J. Laing, *Warriors of the Dark Ages* (Sutton, 2000). The text of Priscus' account of his visit to Attila's court can be found in R. C. Blockley, *The Fragmentary Classicising Historians of the Later Roman Empire* (Francis Cairns, 1983). See also Otto Maenchen-Helfen, *The World of the Huns: studies in their history and culture* (University of California Press, 1973) which deals more fully with their material culture. For a classic but very readable account see Edward Gibbon, *Decline and Fall of the Roman Empire* (numerous editions, Chapters xxxiv and xxxv).

On the early Arab conquests see F.M. Donner, *The Early Muslim Conquests* (Princeton University Press, 1981) and, more generally, H. Kennedy, *The Prophet and the Age of the Caliphates* (Longman, 1986). Still useful is the account by C. H. Becker, 'The Expansion of the Saracens', in *The Cambridge Medieval History* (Cambridge University Press, 1913), pp. 329–90. For the conquest of Iraq see M. Morony, *Iraq after the Muslim Conquests* (Princeton University Press, 1984). For the conquest of Egypt see A. J. Butler, *The Arab Conquest of Egypt*, ed. P. M. Fraser (Oxford University Press, 1978). For Muslim armies in this period see H. Kennedy, *The Armies of the Caliphs* (Routledge, 2001). For military equipment see 'Arms of the Umayyad Era', in ed. Y. Lev, *War and Society in the Eastern Mediterranean* (E. J. Brill, Leiden, 1997), pp. 9–100.

A good account of the history of Central Asia in the early Middle Ages can be found in ed. D. Sinor, *The Cambridge History of Early Inner Asia* (Cambridge University Press, 1990), pp. 285–316. The classic account of the north-eastern frontiers of Iran and the coming of the Turks is V. V. Barthold, *Turkistan down to the Mongol Invasions* (Gibb Memorial Series, London, 1968). For Turkish soldiers in the employ of the 'Abbasid caliphs see M. Gordon, *The Breaking of a Thousand Swords: A History of the Turkish Community of Samarra, 815–889 CE* (Albany, 2001). The Seljuk Turks in Turkey are discussed in C. Cahen, *The Formation of Turkey* (Longman, London, 2001). For the battle of Manzikert see especially J. Haldon, *The Byzantine Wars* (Tempus, 2001), pp. 121–7.

The best introductory account of the Mongols is D. Morgan, *The Mongols* (Blackwell, 1986). A lively and interesting account with excellent illustrations is provided in R. Marshall, *Storm from the East* (BBC Books, London, 1993). For the life of Genghis Khan himself see P. Ratchnevsky, *Genghis Khan: his life and legacy* (trans. T. N. Haining, Blackwell, 1981). *The Secret History of the Mongols* is translated and edited by U. Onon (E. J. Brill, Leiden, 1990). For Juvayni's Persian account, see the English translation by J. A. Boyle, *Genghis Khan: the History of the World Conqueror* (2nd ed., Manchester University Press, 1997). On the Mongol invasions of Europe see J. Chambers, *The Devil's Horsemen; the Mongol Invasion of Europe* (London, 1979). The Mongol invasion of Russia is described in G. Vernadsky, *The Mongols and Russia* (Yale University Press, 1953) and re-evaluated in J. L. I. Fennell, *The Crisis of Medieval Russia, 1200–1304* (Longman, London, 1983).

There is a vast general literature on the Vikings. For a good, well-illustrated general introduction see J. Graham-Campbell, *The Viking World* (Frances Lincoln, London, 1989). Else Roesdahl's *The Vikings* (Penguin Books, London, 1998) is both readable and scholarly. See also P. H. Sawyer, *Kings and Vikings* (Routledge, London, 1996) by one of the leading authorities in the field. For the Vikings from a contemporary point of view see R. I. Page's *Chronicles of the Vikings* (British Museum Press, London, 1995). There are also two accessible and well-illustrated reference works: J. Haywood, *Historical Atlas of the Vikings* (Penguin Books, London, 1995) and, also by J. Haywood, *Encyclopaedia of the Viking Age* (Thames and Hudson, London, 2000).

INDEX

Picture credits

Every effort has been made to contact the copyright holders for images reproduced in this book. The publishers would welcome any errors or omissions being brought to their attention.-

Corbis: Endpapers, pp 140 Francis G. Meyer; 27 Brian A. Vikander; 72, 76–7, 209 Bettmann; 142 Diego Lezama Orezzoli; 146 NASA; 146–7, 162–3 Dean Conger; 150 Hulton-Deutsch Collection; 152 Steffan Widstrand; 172, 178, 180, 200 Ted Spiegel; 213 Adrian Arbib; 100 Corbis. Peter Newark's Pictures pp. 6, 16–17, 159; Art Archive pp.14, 25, 46–7, 49, 66, 81, 104, 111, 176, 189 below, 204–5, 208; Werner Forman Archive pp. 18–19, 20, 63, 69, 102–3, 124, 179, 181, 187, 188, 208; Sonia Halliday Photographs pp. 36 right, 40–41, 51, 52, 56, 75, 168, 206; Bridgeman Art Library: 22 Private Collection; 53 Vatican Museums & Galleries, Italy; 54 Biblioteca Estense, Modena, Italy; 143 British Library. Ancient Art & Architecture Collection pp. 24, 26, 30, 36 left, 50, 64, 66, 128, 160, 161, 164, 210–11; British Museum pp. 28, 29, 38, 95, 100, 107, 116, 119, 123, 124, 131, 139, 198–9; Hutchison Library pp. 32–3, 45, 58–9, 114–5, 115, 149, 174, 190–91; AKG pp. 12, 37, 48, 67, 80, 108, 126, 134–5, 156–7, 158, 183, 184–5, 189 above, 202–3; Author pp. 70–71, 83, 88, 89, 92, 137, 139; Scala pp. 65; Institute of Archaeology pp. 82; Freer Gallery of Art, Washington pp. 96; Crown Copyright pp. 99; Edinburgh University Library pp. 110, 120; National Palace Museum, Taiwan p. 113; Victoria & Albert Museum pp 118; Corpus Christi College, Cambridge p. 125.

Drawings on the title page and on pages 31, 34, 35, 45, 62, 64, 65, 90, 133 and 167 are by Peter Smith and Malcolm Swanston of Arcadia Editions Ltd.

ENDPAPER: *A medieval impression of the battle of Liegnitz, 1241. The army of the Teutonic knights was lured into a charge and then split – half being cut down by the Mongol archers, the other half being crushed by the Mongol heavy calvary. Templar losses were considerable. The Mongols reputedly counted the dead by cutting an ear off each body, sending nine large sacks to Batu in honour of their victory.*